REBOOT YOUR LIFE:

A 12-DAY PROGRAM FOR ENDING STRESS, REALIZING YOUR GOALS, AND BEING MORE PRODUCTIVE

By Paul Gibbons

[This page intentionally left blank]

Table of Contents

Preface

What you will get out of reading this book

Nothing. Not a thing.

But if you do the 3 minutes of daily reading *and* do the 30 or so minutes of daily exercises for twelve days, you will get astonishing results.

Some of those will be:

1) Clarity on what you care most about and how to make time for that

2) Reconnecting with your passion and purpose

3) Learn to use your natural creativity in all areas of your life

4) A life spring clean—getting rid of unwanted baggage

5) Knowing how to realize goals, not just set them

6) Much better personal organization

7) Enhanced productivity and time management

8) Peace of mind and lots less stress

Why Reboot Your Life?!?

Computer owners know that once the beast has been running for a while, the innards get clogged with cyber-sludge and the only solution is a Reboot. Turn it off and on, and then start up the stuff you need. Life is like that also.

Most people make goals and plans, but having coached hundreds of people, I know that those dreams can stall before escape velocity is reached. In rocketry terms, if they don't make orbit, they fall back to earth with a bump. When plans stall, or dreams are forestalled, it take great effort to reconnect with why they mattered, and plan again for their success.

"Reboot" is a crazy-simple process for starting over and relaunching your dreams. It must be done step by step, and some tools make it much easier.

Life coaches offer tremendous value, but typically charge a few thousand dollars. They provide: (1) the process that produces the result; (2) great questions; and (3) great probing, listening, and challenges.

This is a book on how to coach yourself.

Although having a coach is great, the advantage of learning to do this yourself means that whenever you feel out of touch, off-target, disconnected, stressed, overwhelmed, or depressed, you can get to it.

You may feel none of those things now—but life often throws up transitions like promotions, marriage, kids, divorce, new jobs, windfall incomes, and retirement. At each transition, it is worth taking stock. Where am I now? What is next?

"Reboot" is, in other words, a toolkit for self-transformation.

Who is this book for?

I've worked with everyone from CEOs, celebrities, and politicians to administrative assistants, professional poker players, social entrepreneurs, and struggling artists. They all rave about the results.

"I do Reboot religiously every year. I spring into January on

fire and reconnected to my passion and dreams."

"I used to have big inspiring dreams in my twenties, but as I became more successful, I lost track of the big picture and felt as if I were going through the motions. After Reboot, life feels exactly as it did in my twenties."

"Since working through that process, my life has never been the same, and I've never looked back."

"Just the vision- and goal-setting process was worth its weight in gold."

"The transitions of the last two years were really hard, especially coming one after another. I needed a fresh start, and working through the process gave me much more value than I expected."

"I had a lot of great things in my life, but I still woke up some days thinking 'What's the point?' I needed to reconnect with the big picture: why I was on the planet, what I cared about, and what I was doing to do about that."

I cannot think of anybody who would not benefit from doing an exercise such as this from time to time. Nobody has all of these life-critical conversations 100 percent "cooked" all of the time. The most effective people I know are revisiting and revising them often. So the answer to "who" is: everybody!

You might never have done anything like this; or, you may have done goal-setting at work, but not elsewhere; or, you might have worked through something like this in coaching, but would like to do it on your own; or, you might already do some of this, but need structure, tools, and a comprehensive way to do it. Wherever you are, whether you are a beginner or an experienced hand at "leading yourself," *Reboot!* will give you the boost you want.

When is the process most valuable?

This process began as way to bring in a New Year with refreshed goals, plans, and vision, and to put the missteps from the previous year firmly in the past. The great advantage of doing it then is that most people take time off and workplaces are less busy. The New Year is also, symbolically, a good place to make a fresh start.

Here are some other times:

1) In transitions: divorce, retirement, promotion, big move, kids leaving
2) When overwhelmed and stressed by the number of your commitments
3) When it feels as if lots of junk has accumulated (material, emotional, spiritual)
4) When you feel insanely busy, but also that you are not getting anywhere
5) When considering a big move (career or other), and want to put it in context of your whole life (How will this affect different areas about which I care?)

Better with others

This process works terrifically when done in isolation as an individual. It also works very well (with some modifications) for businesses and for families.

At the very least, you should share important discoveries with people a few times during the process. It would be absurd, for example, to go through all twelve days without sharing with your partner.

The more you talk, the more you bring your reflections and hard work into reality.

If you do this with heart, people will be inspired by your vision and goals and want to help.

Share what you are up to, and if sharing is difficult for you, the value will be multiplied.

Why did I write this book?

Because these tools were transformational in my own life. When I use them, I prosper and flourish. When I fail to, I struggle. In summary, I love this process and so does everyone who has done it!

Here is what it did for me: I was dealt a pretty good hand intellectually, but an awful one in other respects. I am pathologically scatterbrained, unfocused, and forgetful. That I have been able to harness my talents at all has been the result of very hard work on my Achilles' heel: personal effectiveness.

Left to my own devices, I scatter my attention and do what is in front of my face, not what is most important. I start a million things and bounce from one to another. My scatter-brain comes up with tons of ideas, but then the weight of undeveloped ideas, unfinished projects, and unfulfilled ambition can be soul-crushing.

What I needed to do for myself, to address this shortfall, became so powerful and popular that people have repeatedly encouraged me to write it down.

Each year I get e-mails from people who have hit "PBs" in their personal and working lives—launching a business, or running a marathon, or dropping three pants sizes. There are people who twenty years after doing this process with me, have said (and continue to say), "My life has been completely different since."

This book is my invitation to you to join them!

Day 0 – Getting ready

It is no use frantically climbing the ladder of success when it is leaning against the wrong wall. —Steven Covey

Leading yourself

When it comes to the arc of your life, leading is a sacred responsibility. It is also a gift, that of living in a time and place where choices are available to us. We do not face the bone-crushing poverty of Bangladesh or the North American inner city.

Casting that gift aside is, in my view, a sacrilege.

"A life is a terrible thing to waste."

Self-coaching is a way of grabbing the arc of your life and *reclaiming authorship of your destiny.*

The story "I have no time"—for exercise, for recreation, to participate fully in my kids' lives, to spend time adoring my spouse, to start a business, to write a book—is about the unhappiest story of them all. There are the same 168 hours in the week for book-writers and dream-livers and spouse-adorers—they have simply chosen those commitments and said no to others.

Enriching an already great life

Leading yourself requires that you become a self-coach. Self-coaching is not just for people who feel the ache of an unlived life. Very successful and very happy people sometimes let areas slip and dreams fade. I have known great business leaders who are prosperous and respected by their communities, shoot scratch golf, and read great books, but have given up on looking for someone to share that with.

Even the very best, most successful people can have an Achilles' heel, some part of living the dream that is slipping by.

One enriching practice is to look at ways that an already amazing life can be improved. Some people add hobbies, some romance, some vacation and rest, some public service, some extending their education, or some enhancing their career. For example, one year, while using this process, I noticed that I was not being of service in the civic or public sphere. I had no previous political experience or interest (except moaning about politics and politicians). Some friends had suggested I might run for Parliament one day, so I decided, with reservations, to peer over the political fence.

I joined a political party and got involved in policy discussions. By the end of the year, I had had discussions with a dozen Members of Parliament and the leaders of my new party (the equivalent of the Minority Leader in the US). I was most star struck by my meeting with Baroness Shirley Williams, who had negotiated with Mao, Mandela, FW de Klerk, and Brezhnev in her role as Foreign Secretary. (She was the UK's Henry Kissinger in the 1970s.) All this was birthed out of a few hours' reflection at the beginning of a year. While it is doubtful I will ever run for office, my life was deeply enriched by this experience.

My personal giddiness may not excite you, but in my view, everyone has scope to enrich their lives.

The spoils go to those who dare to begin.

Self-leadership and business leadership

Much of my work during the last twenty years has involved developing senior business people in leadership programs. There is a skills portion of leadership development, but leadership experts largely agree on one thing: leadership comes from within (and isn't just about skills). In other words, you cannot lead people effectively unless you're "living the dream" yourself. Having a life in which you realize your potential inspires people to realize theirs, to fight for big dreams, to start companies, go the extra kilometer, and take great risks.

A leader grappling with stress, conflict, unrealized hopes, and too many commitments will lack power, even if she is very good at getting her "game face" on. With the results of the Reboot process in her back pocket, however, and with a foundation of authenticity and integrity, she can tap into new power.

No program that I run for senior executives begins without a process like this, because to work on their leadership, they need a clean slate (or one in the process of being cleaned).

Why is this different than New Year's resolutions?

In 2003, I was moving house with a new wife, Cari, and a baby on the way. Cari was emptying drawers and she came across a two-page document called "Paul's 1999 goals."

The goals were big, and there were a lot of them, including starting a business, finding a relationship, getting a master's degree, getting certified as a coach, becoming debt-free, running a 10k, meditating and doing yoga, and starting to write. People achieve much more than that in a lifetime, but in the mid-1990s, although I had an amazing job, my life looked like the aftermath of Hurricane Katrina. Running a trading desk at an investment bank in the 1980s had earned me a ton of money, but the hedonistic 'lifestyle' (a euphemism) had nearly destroyed me. Miserable, I knew there was more to life than money, but I had no idea how to get whatever that was.

How then do you "get a life"? I read everything I could, but the most transformative was Steven Covey's *Seven Habits of Highly Effective People*. He talked about things like mission, vision, values, goals, priorities and discipline – which were, for me, completely alien concepts.

Following Covey's prescription, I had written the goals in January 1999, and by December 1999, they were all achieved or well underway. What is amazing here is that I spent two days thinking about them, wrote them once, and never looked at them again. As if by magic, I found myself insanely busy but doing the right things often enough so as to create a miraculous year.

Lots of people set goals at New Year's and call them resolutions. Fewer than 25 percent of resolutions make it into February. What was I doing right?

Here is $100,000 answer: You cannot make new commitments, or dream new dreams, or start afresh in any way without "completing" what is already in place—that's like trying to build a beautiful temple on a garbage dump. "Completing" might not mean finishing everything. (It would be pretty silly coaching advice to say, "Finish everything you are working on, then we will start living some dreams.") When you enumerate the obstacles that are in your way and your current commitments, however, some things will be discarded and some will be postponed, but in a conscious manner and for the sake of bigger things.

I don't live in the fantasy that you can, today, start from a blank piece of paper. Your life is already a network of commitments to family, friends, employers, and your community. What is often true, though, is that some commitments need to be pruned, some revitalized, and some new ones invented. By doing that, you create the space for great things (things you say you want) to happen.

A new life in twelve 30-minute steps

A journey of 100 miles begins with a simple step—and this process tells you exactly what steps to take.

The process requires 30 minutes each day. There is reading, writing, and reflection in varying proportions every day. Reading is always the smallest portion, taking 3 to 5 minutes maximum. Writing will vary between 5 and 15 minutes, and reflection will take the rest. On most days, most of the process will involve thinking about your life.

There are 365 days in a year and 168 hours in a week. This entire process takes six hours, or a quarter of a day. For that tiny fraction of investment—3 percent of one week, or .07 percent of a year—the returns are bountiful.

You will need to commit that 30 minutes each day, but in my

experience people who devote that time (or get close to it) get a new lease on life and new energy, and they start making progress in areas where they were stopped or struggling. There is writing each day, but the writing portion takes only about 10 percent of the time required. You are cheating yourself if you do one of the exercises in 3 or 10 minutes, because what matters most here is the time you spend *thinking* and *feeling* the exercise. The more you put into this, the more you get out.

If you cannot find that time on a particular day, do not shortchange yourself and skimp. Pull out tomorrow's calendar and place an indelible-ink appointment to work on the step you missed. Give yourself a day off and do not beat yourself up over it.

Decide when you are going to spend your 30 daily minutes now. Research shows that if commitments are linked to a trigger, such as "when I take my lunch break," "after I drop the kids at soccer," or "right before *The X Factor*," they are less likely to be forgotten. Be rigorous now and put those 30-minute blocks in your calendar or timekeeping system.

Simple, but not easy

One mental obstacle that gets in the way of people's success (generally and with this process) is confusing something being conceptually "simple" with being "easy" to execute. There is no Einsteinian theory of general relativity that transforms lives. Sorry. The knowledge I'm about to bestow upon you is not that complicated. Most third graders could complete the exercises herein.

What makes the real difference is persistence, discipline, and follow-through. For many people (including me), those things are more difficult than general relativity.

If you get stuck at some point, ask for help (you can email me), or power through the stuck place. If you drop this for a month, do not let the fact that you missed thirty-one days prevent you from picking it up on the thirty-second. If, having made a solemn promise to do something, you find yourself doing the opposite, stop, make peace with yourself, and get back on the path.

Shortcuts

Although this process works best as a whole, some people will want to cherry-pick. If you do, you will potentially miss great insights in areas that you don't know that you don't know about—your blind spots.

Nevertheless, the table below will give you a guide to cherry-picking, which I hope you don't use.

Where you are	Relevant days
Stressed, overwhelmed, disconnected	Days 1 through 5
Lacking inspiration and direction	Days 6 through 8
Needing focus, clarity, and direction	Days 7 through 10
Managing time, renewing commitments	Days 11 and 12

Where you get the value

Different people get value from different days. Some rate every single day 10/10 for value, some give a mixture of 8s and 7s for it all, some give eight 10s and four 2s. Do it all, but if a particular day does not seem to give you what you expected, plough on for two reasons. The first is obvious. If one day does not do it for you, and you guillotine the entire process you might miss the few days that would make a transformational difference to you. The second reason is more subtle. You may not feel the results of a day the minute you put down a pen. People constantly say "I've been thinking about my reflections on day X for a week, and I have finally realized an important truth." It is possible, even likely, that you wake up a week after doing something and notice "Hey, I feel completely different! How did that happen?"

Technology and Reboot

My website has a special section devoted to Reboot! There is space to give feedback on your experience, share stories, and to sign-up to get updates, and free tools. By mid-2014, there will be a webinar series to support "Rebooters". Please see www.paulgibbons.net/RebootYourLife for details.

We are going to be doing a lot of writing, reflection and list-making. Each day builds on the reflections and writing of the previous day so we need a way to capture that. There are three options, one paper and two digital.

Solution 1: Paper

To use the paper version, you will need to make copies of or **print**

out the templates at the end of the book. There are ten of them (for days one through ten).

Advantages: Many people (even today) find that writing personal things (plans, dreams, and ideas) by hand comes more easily than typing them.

Disadvantages: The weakness of this (besides environmental) is that written information is harder to move around, sort, and update.

Solution 2: Excel

There is a single Excel workbook available at www.paulgibbons.net/RebootYourLife with a tab for each day. After entering your email address, you'll receive worksheets 5 minutes later. You will also get revisions and additions completely free, as well as access to other tools you will find on my website.

Advantages: Data can be moved around, sorted, and refreshed easily.

Disadvantages: Some people may find typing their vision or mission into a spreadsheet arid and uninspiring, or may be otherwise technologically challenged.

Solution 3: Evernote

Evernote is free and perhaps the most useful personal organizing technology ever invented (ok, perhaps the calendar but that was a while ago!) Each day, we receive multiple inputs (voicemails, texts, e-mails, web pages, print media, Post-it notes, etc.)—and we need a single place where *all* of that can be categorized and accessed. We also have multiple devices (phones, tablets, laptops and desktops). **Any information about personal management has to be available wherever you are and whenever you need it.** If you make a to-do list on your phone while sitting at the airport, you want it waiting there for you when you open up your laptop at home to do the work. If you make a list of people to call on your PC, you want it available on your phone when it's time to make the calls. Evernote syncs multiple inputs across multiple devices and has outstanding search and sort features.

Evernote is the best long-term solution. In Appendix 2, you'll find a list of Evernote "notes" that you will need. (Don't worry, these are created day-to-day, not all at once.)

Now to begin!

"Whatever you can do or dream you can, begin it. Boldness has genius, power and magic in it!"

—Goethe

Our process

This is what the next twelve days will look like.

Day	The day's mission	
0	*Preparing to coach yourself to greatness*	*Introduction*
I	*Domains of success*	*Cleaning house. Getting out from under stress, overwhelm, and debris.*
II	*The rug*	
III	*The runway*	
IV	*Clearing the rug and the runway*	
V	*An attitude of gratitude*	
VI	*Your mission in life*	*Getting clear on the big picture of your life.*
VII	*Your five-year vision*	
VIII	*Setting inspiring goals*	*Gaining clarity, focus and traction.*
IX	*Turning goals into projects*	
X	*Turning projects into next actions*	*Managing your time and keeping this process alive.*
XI	*Deciding what to do when*	
XII	*Keeping this going—for the rest of your life*	

Day 1 – Domains of your success

I want to die young. At 80.

—Anonymous

When I was twenty a friend got married, and naturally his mother, who was sixty-five, flew in for the celebrations. When I met her, I fell in love—not romantically, but with how this woman lived her life. I only spent a few hours in her company, but I remember her vividly still, thirty years later. She was teaching school, doing a PhD, and running for local office, she danced longer and harder than the twenty-year-olds, and she was dating a new beau back home. I wanted to say "Hey, don't you know you are sixty-five?" (Sixty-five is *really* old when you are twenty.)

What has stayed with me to this day is not just her vitality but also the breadth of her interests and activities, as well as the scale of her ambitions in each of her important areas. There was not a whiff of resignation about her, nor a whiff of "it is too late for that."

That brief meeting changed how I view success in life. I believe we prosper not just through depth, but also through cultivating a breadth of activities and making a commitment to live each area of life to the fullest. It saddens me greatly when I work with thirty to fifty-somethings who have lost touch with past loves (hobbies or passions), and I always nudge them in the direction of picking up something that they'll do not for money, not to make other people happy, and not for recognition, but purely for its own sake. One early writer on personal growth, Scott Peck, thought such pursuits were "the means through which we love ourselves."

Socrates said that the unexamined life was not worth living. I counter that the unlived life is not worth examining!

We are going to create a list of areas of our lives that matter deeply to us. This list varies a lot from person to person, but some concerns are standard for most 21st century people:

➢ Well-being, health
➢ Finances
➢ Family
➢ Education
➢ Primary relationship
➢ Friends
➢ Home (the house or apartment)
➢ Career
➢ Job

There are also others that matter more or less to different people:

➢ Hobbies
➢ Sports
➢ Travel
➢ Spirituality
➢ Church
➢ Community service
➢ Politics
➢ Cultural enrichment (could be travel, could be art, could be WWF)
➢ Fun (you can be creative here too!)

And you can also have areas that are quite specific examples:

- ➤ Habitat for Humanity service
- ➤ PTA role
- ➤ Golf league
- ➤ Soccer coach
- ➤ International travel
- ➤ Cottage in Michigan
- ➤ Taking care of parents

In one sense, you are "just" going to make a list, but there is a huge trap here: making this list is **not a descriptive process, but rather a creative one**. What do I mean?

You already have five or six things you care about: a job, friends, and maybe children, hobbies, and school. There is *some* value in listing those and setting goals, but the gold is to be found by looking more broadly and creatively. By creating a new category, you declare that you are going to pay attention to that category in a new way.

Some examples are:

1)   You may not have a category called health or finance, but there are minimum levels of attention needed to live well (and long), and very high levels of excellence are possible in such categories.

2)   You may have other neglected areas. I sometimes find very successful people who neglect (not willfully) friendships or extended family due to their busyness.

3)   Adding an area can enrich your life. Perhaps "culture" (maybe Bieber, maybe WWF, maybe Wagner, or crafts fairs/ museums). Perhaps "being of service, or "learning something just

for the sake of learning it", or picking up a new hobby (or reconnecting with an old one).

4)   There might be "stuff you just do" where you would be inspired by a new level of achievement or focus. Play golf? Take five shots off your game. Kids like sports or music? Find them the best instruction you can. Married? Make "Spouse" a category and make that category inspirational (to them). Enriching an area might be adding an absurdly distant goal (like me doing a 10k when my previous best distance was a 100m.)

5)   You should have at least two work categories: "Career" and "Job." Career is the management of your long-term productive activities, which will include (at least) skills building, brand building, networking, and having a plan for either your next promotion or retirement. "Job," meanwhile, is an uninspiring description, so choose another one that is more descriptive. If you are a "portfolio person" (as I am), you may have several. I have "Writer" and "Consultant" categories now. When I ran a company, I had "Chairman" and "Rainmaker" categories, with different goals in each.

Your turn now! Use the worksheet at the back of this book, or the spreadsheet or Evernote you have ready to go.

What you need to do

Part A: Make a list of the areas that matter to you the most. You will only write down seven to twelve "domains of success," but this should take you at least 15 minutes if you give it the reflection time needed.

Part B: Rate each area on a scale of 1 to 10 in the next column. Go with your gut, but take off the rose-colored glasses if you wear those, and take of the mud-stained glasses if you wear those. (There are people for whom "okay" actually means "horrible," and people for whom "horrible" actually means "okay.")

Part C: In each area, jot down a few words or a sentence that answers the question, "What does a "10" look like?" (This should also take about 15 minutes.)

Congratulations! We are on our way.

Day 2 – The rug

As life progresses, baggage can accumulate. Goals are set but abandoned. Projects are started but sit idle. Promotions may not happen. Circumstances may not fit with our expectations. We bump up against people and harbor resentment. Bad choices can lead to regret. Certain areas of our lives can be in disarray.

Anxious to go on to more pleasant things, those mishaps get brushed under the rug. They can be ignored—but only for a while.

For example, my dream has long been to write. Although I'd had many articles published, I had not written a book, and had several unfinished ones on my computer. So when a potentially exciting new project popped into mind, my excitement about the idea was quickly crushed by the shadow and weight of those unfinished projects. Similarly, if your garage or attic is a dumping ground, then each time you walk in, there is a momentary dissatisfaction. If you have been ignoring health or financial issues that need attention, those can slow you down. Every time the door opens on a disorderly area, a slight "thud" checks your stride.

The stuff under the rug is "incomplete." An "incompletion" takes up psychic energy—even when we give such matters no direct thought, they weigh upon our enthusiasm and our mood. To be maximally creative, inspired, and energetic, we cannot afford to carry around past baggage.

Today, we are going to make a list of everything that is

incomplete for you. This is the time to be painstakingly thorough. Do not worry that making this list will oblige you to take a month off to fix everything. Some things you will fix instantly, this week. Some things you will never fix, but you will promise yourself to be at peace with that. Some things, which fall in the middle, will go on a list of things to do in the near future. Some things will be put on hold on what David Allen calls a "Someday-Maybe" list—but they will be written down, and you will get to them when the time is right.

> **"You are letting go of the small stuff, so you can do the big stuff."**

One huge advantage of writing all these things down is that you no longer have to waste energy remembering them. When you walk into the messy garage, you can be at peace knowing it is on your list and will be handled.

This activity sometimes first produces a slump in the shoulders and a grunt. It all feels like too much. How did life get so complex?! But somewhere between the end of this process and when we start to shift all of this, 100 percent of the people who do it begin to feel lighter. And lighter. And then they're ready for lift-off. When I have a lot of unfinished business *not* written down is when life is most difficult. It's as if a black cloud is following me around. I know there is a lot of "stuff" out there, but I'm not clear what it is or when that "stuff" might hit the fan. Writing it down produces instant relief. For me, worries, cares, and concerns begin to disappear when I look them squarely in the face. Long before I actually do anything about them, I feel better. Clarity becomes my new best friend.

What to do now

Using the template for Day 2 (either at the back of this book, or in the downloaded worksheets), write down your list of everything that is incomplete for you.

Great work! We are not going to let this list fester, but that is all for today. Over the next twenty-four hours, when one of the "mental or emotional" items comes up—a resentment, a regret, or self-judgment—make a conscious effort to just let it go. Say, "I'm going to let that one go." Remind yourself of why: because it is holding you back from bigger things.

Day 3 – The runway

David Allen uses the metaphor of the runway in his writing and teaching, which is very apt. In order to soar at 30,000 feet, you need a clear runway for takeoff. Unlike some self-development gurus, Allen believes that if you are to consider big-picture things like mission, vision, and values, you cannot have a head full of "stuff" occupying your attention. I share his view. A process for systematically "capturing the things that are capturing your attention" is essential before lifting one's sights to the horizon.

On Day 2, we looked mostly backward—at what items from the past might be a drag preventing lift-off. Today, Day 3, we will look at today and the future.

We are going to do something David Allen calls a mindsweep (although it has been around with many different names for a very long time, the word "mindsweep" captures the essence beautifully). The idea is to get everything else that is on your mind **out of your head** and onto paper. The more stuff you carry around in your head—to-dos, projects, conversations, errands, stuff to fix, appointments to keep—the less free your head is for thinking, creativity, and inspiration (leadership, in other words).

First, you need to learn to use mind mapping. Look at the following example mind map, which is from Tony Buzan, the inventor of the tool. This particular mind map describes what mind maps are and how they work.

The why and how of mind maps

The mind does not create neat little outline structures (Point I, Subpoint A, Sub-Subpoint *i*, etc.) People remember things non-sequentially, or organically. Mind mapping is a great tool for planning, outlining, facilitating, note-taking, and many other things. It is trivially simple to learn, and it produces great benefits. All you need to do is draw a circle in the middle of a sheet of paper and start filling in branches with whatever pops into your head. There, you've learned it!

To use mind mapping for a mindsweep, get the biggest sheet of paper you can get your hands on and write down the first commitment, worry, task, dream, vision, project, relationship, phone call, errand, or whatever that pops into your head. Then do the next one. Don't concern yourself too much with grouping, but if you find yourself writing down a number of errands, then create a branch called "errands." If something unrelated pops into mind, make another branch or add it to another one you've already created.

Here is a list of triggers David Allen suggests using. Go through each trigger, see what pops into mind, and mindmap it.

Paper, notes, receipts, reminders in bags, piles, and drawers	Work projects	People to talk to
Things that need to be fixed	Appointments to make	Projects you haven't started/projects you've abandoned
Stuff around the house/in your car	Things you would love to do	Customers/clients/staff
Upcoming events to prepare for	Stuff related to finance	Community/civic activity
Bucket list items	Errands	Hobbies/fun stuff/family stuff

The greatest thing about mindsweeps is you can do them anytime you have a pen and a piece of paper and want to dump all the stuff that is keeping your head busy and your body stressed. Software makes pretty mind maps but can somewhat impede the spontaneity and free-flowing nature of them. Although I sometimes use software for mindsweeps, my preference is a piece of paper larger than 8 ½" x 11" (A4 in Europe) so I don't feel constrained by the paper size and can get it *all* down.

Most important tip for this stage of the process: Do *not* get sucked into doing anything on this list right now unless it involves a single motion (like casting something into the trash). The first time you do this, you want to devote at least 20 minutes to simply emptying your head. You will likely start with many items per minute, but slow down as you go—be thorough and persevere. You want a list that you are fairly certain has everything on it. The more you trust that list, the clearer your head will be of clutter.

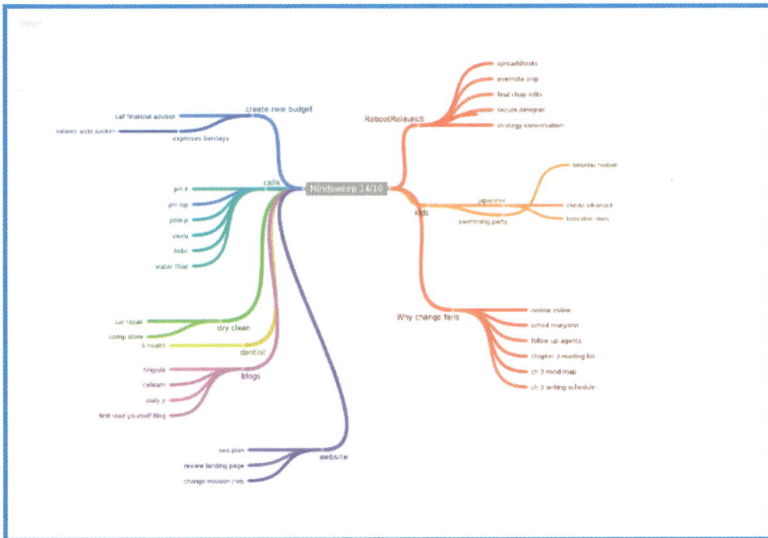

Example of a mindsweep

Day 4 – Clearing the rug and the runway

We now have an enormous list from Days 2 and 3 (it wouldn't be unusual to have as many as one hundred items), and we need to figure out how all that stuff gets handled—off of paper and on to making a difference in your life. To do this, we are going to categorize it into a series of different lists.

There are five ways you are going to categorize all that stuff, four Ds and one P: **DUMP, DEFER, PLAN, DO, DELEGATE.** Some version of this list is found in every book on personal organization, but this is the version that I prefer.

Dump

While "Dump" sounds simple, many people find letting go of something challenging. A nasty cognitive bias called the "sunk cost fallacy" means people focus too much on what they've put into something and not what they might get out of it. This bias keeps people in bad jobs ("but I've been here twelve years"), bad relationships ("he/she will change, I'm sure"), moneypit houses ("just another $7k and nothing else can go wrong"), and bad investments ("my broker says we will get our money back one day"). The truth is, **you cannot recover that time (or money), and the only obligation you have is to the future, not the past.** So be ruthless to be kind.

"In some ways, life is like a cup: you can't pour great things

in until you make some room."

If you have something on this scale to get rid of, it will take some effort. One thing that will help is to imagine what you would say to a close friend in the same situation. Another is the vision exercise on Day 7 that we will use to develop and enhance your view of what "great" looks like. It is easier to let go of the past when you have a clear, emotionally rich picture of what the future could be like.

Emotions, such as resentment and regret, can also be hard to let go of. Anger is natural, but short-lived. Resentment, its ugly twin, can live on for decades, hurting the "resenter" much more than the "resentee." Maybe that old relationship "done you wrong," but you can choose whether that affects future ones. Occasional sadness is natural, but regret (coulda, woulda, shoulda) is a lack of peace with the past that affects your ability to make choices in the present. Beating yourself up about not finishing your MBA was fun before, perhaps, but you can't do it forever!

Many people start things with enthusiasm but find them hard to finish. Maybe rebuilding a 1973 T-Bird or creating a website for orphaned Siamese cats seemed a good idea at the time, but no longer does. If a project will not serve the future you, then put it down.

Letting go is not always easy, but it *always* begins with becoming willing to do so and then saying it. You might second-guess yourself while letting go of something big, but remember why you are letting go of it in the first place. If it reappears, let it go again. You are done.

Defer (and the "Someday-Maybe" list)

David Allen, the productivity guru, invented the "Someday-Maybe" list, which is worth its weight in gold. When we defer something, we are going to put it on that list. On my "S-M" list I have long-term dreams (like "bucket list" items), ideas for books and articles that I might someday get to, projects that are important but which I've had to shift to the back burner, niggling things that I do not want to forget (such as a car service), and things to read, study, and listen to when I get the time.

"Time management is just as much about what you are NOT doing as what you ARE doing."

The power of the "S-M" list is in the fact that it gives you a place to put both "Hawaii vacation" and "Plan 20th anniversary"—that is, a dream you may never realize (but why not?), and something you darned well better do but do not have time to do now. The "S-M" list's power also comes from having something separate from your "to-do" list, allowing that list to be focused purely on what you are committed to doing right away.

This clears your mind for other critical things. To put it in neuroscience terms, your "working memory" is freed up, which improves focus and concentration.

Plan (and the "Projects" list)

If it requires more than a few actions, it is a project. Your Projects list should include things like getting old family VHS tapes digitized, researching, planning, and booking a family vacation, writing a book (which can be an 18-month project with lots of sub-projects), creating a world-class resume, preparing a presentation for your boss, finding a ballet teacher for your daughter, or doubling the size of your professional network. On Day 9 we'll look at how you create and manage personal projects, but for now we are just going to create a "Projects" list that contains all our multi-step items.

Do

If it takes "a sec" (meaning under 2 minutes), we can just do it or put it on a list. To begin with, I recommend the list. There is a huge trap here—stuff that looks quick and easy can hijack this categorization process. Even "collect expense receipts" can turn into a 30-minute excursion by itself. Be really strict, because we want to get through your whole "rug" and "runway"—but if you can trust yourself to quickly send that email without being tempted to respond to fifty others once you are in your email program, then by all means do it and cross it off.

Delegate

On your "Delegate" list, write down who will do it, when you are going to ask, and when you are going to ask them to finish it.

Important tip: Do not be afraid to dump things or defer

("someday-maybe") them. Most people do not have vast swaths of time waiting in their lives for enriching, valuable, and creative things. They are more often overwhelmed and stressed—and part of that overwhelm comes from doing too many of the wrong things.

What you need to do now

Start the first step in today's process (either using the template in Appendix 1 or the downloaded Excel spreadsheet or your Evernote notebook). List all your rug/runway items in the leftmost column, then quickly go through your list and put an "x" beside them in the correct category (Dump, Defer, Project, Do, or Delegate).

The second step in the process is to create five fresh lists: DUMP, SOMEDAY-MAYBE (DEFER), PROJECTS (PLAN), DO, and DELEGATE. After you have done this, your lists from Days 2 and 3 should be empty.

The third and final step today is to schedule some time to go through your DO list. This can be extremely fulfilling, because in 30 minutes, if you're focused, you can plough through ten or more items. This is because the list contains many things that you can do quickly.

You may be thinking, "Jeepers, I'm out of the frying pan and into the fire, here. I may know what I need to do, but what an absurd number of lists!"

Here is why you need them all: One thing that stops people from being productive is when they have lists that contain items of different complexity, urgency, importance, and duration. In contrast, if I have a list that includes only things that I can do quickly, I can grab 30 minutes and power through them. If (less usefully) that list includes big and little, urgent and non-urgent tasks, such as, "Create strategic marketing plan for 2014," "Balance last six bank statements," "Buy stamps," and "Confront kid about "C" grade on test," it is less attractive to pick up.

Continue to power through your "Do" list during the next eight days.

Where to next?

We have now taken four days to mostly look backward and get stuff out of the way and off your mind so that your mind can be clear for the next four days.

As we continue to work, continue to populate your lists if new things come into your head. You will probably find yourself with more creative ideas than usual. Write them down! Put them on your "Someday-Maybe" list for now.

Day 5 – An attitude of gratitude

Feeling gratitude and not expressing it is like wrapping a present and not giving it. (William Arthur Ward)

Building on gratitude, not on wants

Now we are going to create a gratitude list.

Why gratitude? In designing a new future, we do not want to base it on a foundation of lack, of complaint, of suffering, or of comparison. In coming days, we are going to envision a different future, and the most solid basis for that is an open and grateful heart.

Not only will it make our process work, but it is not a bad place to live from. Do this, and the next twenty-four hours will look different to you!

Entitlement, the opposite of gratitude

It is easy to go through life looking at what we don't have, comparing our life with ideals, achievements, and standards of others. Consider the old joke, "How much is a good salary?" to which the answer is, "10 percent more than your brother-in-law." It is easy, I know, to go through life more "present" to complaints, issues, problems, grouches, and the rest.

Everyone does this to some extent some of the time. On occasion, when my life has been tough, those negatives have been all I have been present to. Every great, wonderful, fantastic thing always has a *but* attached when I am in that mood. Grasping for gratitude, I might turn my head from the bleakness toward the light and say, "Well, my (kids, health, work) are great"—but the *buts* interject, and back to staring at the abyss I go.

Even when things are going superbly well, that can be taken for granted. Life's bounties are not seen with a grateful heart (partly because of a dark tunnel called "entitlement").

Gratitude and leadership

Those words may seem a strange combination, but consider the orientation of someone who lives from gratitude. It predisposes toward generosity and giving. Lack, or entitlement, predisposes toward grasping and taking.

People like to follow givers and not takers. I founded a very successful company on a very powerful vision and an orientation toward serving the world and clients. However, as times got tough, my anxieties and stresses made me worry more about what I was getting. (Would I recover financially my investment of time and capital into the company? Would we survive the recession?) The more I worried, the more my orientation toward cherished colleagues and clients became "What can I get here?"—and trust, relationships, and performance suffered.

A grateful leader attracts followers, a grasping leader pushes them away.

The gratitude list

Before you begin: The trap here is not just to report a generic list with no emotional connection. So don't woodenly write "I am grateful for my family," say who, for what, and how: "I am grateful for Conor, a healthy, loving son, growing up mindful and wise"; "I am grateful to my sister for her support during my divorce"; "I am grateful for the amazing vacation I took this year." This helps us get "present" to the mood of gratitude and not just reeling off stuff. **Specifics** make this personal and emotional. When you write it, feel it!

Part A: Now list *fifty* things you are grateful for. The length of the list is not an invitation to trivialize. You should spent 25 minutes doing this, and really concentrate on **being present** and **feeling it** as you do it.

Part B: Share your gratitude. When I do this with people in coaching sessions, their lists are either mostly people or all people. It seems (rightfully) that people are more grateful for people than for things! The gratitude exercise is immensely more powerful if you tell them. It does not have to be a speech or "done right," just a heartfelt "I am really glad you are in my life." Put a date next to all the people for whom you are grateful, and then call them. If one of them has passed away, perhaps spend a minute or two remembering them in gratitude.

Day 6 – Your mission in life

The "perfect time" never arrives for big dreams. The storm, called life, through which you sail has no calm eye. You never will, by magic, get an extra twenty hours a week. Start now! (Paul Gibbons)

Where we are going now

During the next five days, we are going to be designing an inspiring future for you. The structure of this process is depicted in the following diagram. The top of the pyramid has the longest timescales: a mission is usefully thought of as lasting a lifetime, a vision a few years, goals about a year, projects from a few weeks to a few months, and next actions you will do within a week to ten days.

Mission

Vision

Goals

Projects

Next Actions

Creating your mission in life

Having a mission in life can provide a sense of power and purpose to everything you do. A mission is a deep, life-shaping stand you take. It announces to the world what you care about and to what you dedicate your life. There is a trap here, of thinking it must be something world-changing and noble (Gandhi-esque). As you will see in the examples below, it can be something very close to home. The more specific it is to you, the better.

Good news: you already have one! Since you began adulthood, certain principles, stands, commitments, and values have been there. Our job is partly creative, but partly also to try to make sense of what has been driving you historically.

So why do the exercise if you, as I maintain, already have one? The questions below will provoke thinking and reflection on the arc of your life: what has gone before and what is yet to come. Codifying your mission in a very few sentences provides clarity for you, and gives you a way to talk about yourself, your passions, and your interests that is not about you. (Because while a mission is written by you, it should not be about you, but rather about what you offer to the world and your communities.)

Guidelines

Today's template has some questions to guide you through the process, but here are some more guidelines:

1) It must be utterly specific to you and could have been written by nobody else.
2) It must focus on what you give to life and not what you get.
3) It should (ideally) include more than just work.

Examples

Here are some example mission statements. See if you can guess which one is mine!

I heal people through the practice of medicine and through the quality of the medical care and emotional caring they receive. My general practice is special because we focus holistically on well-being (while eschewing holistic medicine), and we work hardest at preventing illness before it starts. But mostly wellness and prosperity begin at home, and my husband and children feel the care most deeply.

I elevate the most important conversations in the world by writing, teaching, scholarship, and bringing creative ideas where they are needed. My work integrates science, philosophy, and business, transforms lives and businesses, and helps shape a better future for the planet. When not having fun doing the work I love, I love raising two amazing boys and living a full, passionate life.

I bring all of myself to my role as an administrative assistant, growing in what I offer each year and being an example to my boss of a stress-free, balanced, and organized life. In three years, my legal assistant qualification will allow me to make a bigger difference, and to better provide for my children. Away from career and home, I serve the community through helping with political campaigns and working on the PTA.

Creating your mission statement

Turn now to the worksheet for today (in Appendix 1) and work through the questions. As you answer questions, you'll see a picture of the whole and common themes begin to emerge. It might be ideal to start this in the morning, carry it around for a day, and complete it in the evening. Do not worry if it does not come out perfectly cooked the first time—it may well take shape over the next few days.

Day 7 – Your five-year vision

The thing about overnight success is that it takes about fifteen years.

—Various

A vision is an emotional, visual, and cognitive picture of what the good life looks like to you. Whether you have formally written one down or not, you already have one. When someone says "You should open a Szechuan restaurant" and you say "Nope," it is because you already have a vision of what great looks like. When choices present themselves, you hold them up side by side with your picture of "the good": that picture is your vision.

So why, if you already have one, write it down? Two reasons: clarity and breadth. Writing it down forces you to ask the tough questions of yourself and to make sure you cover all the important areas with the **clarity** they produce. To create a robust life, you need a **broad** vision that includes all most important areas, not just Chinese restaurants: a picture of a great career, relationship, family life, health, hobbies, and community. The vision process clarifies and articulates what you care about in a useful way.

What else does your vision do? It **inspires**, **directs**, and **aligns**.

Vision inspires. Vision makes your spirit soar. When you look at your vision, say of December 2014, of what life will look like—of what you will have realized, of which dreams will have come true, and which will be in progress—you should shout, "Yeah, baby, bring it!" (Or, if like me you are from England, you might quietly say, "That sounds quite enticing").

Vision directs. My vision includes writing a *New York Times* bestseller on business leadership (a vision is no place to play small). When faced with choices, I can ask, "Will this be a step toward that, or an impediment?" or "Does this activity support my big commitments, or does it distract from them?" Visions bring the big picture into view; part of my vision is to be fitter and leaner, to be a great dad, and to prosper financially, so when faced with a career choice, I have a sense of how that choice affects other things I care about.

Vision aligns. Everybody needs followers and I do not mean the Twitter kind (although they are a subset of the followers I mean). Running a business, running for office, selling products and services, changing the world—whatever game you are playing, you need people playing on your team. If you craft your vision correctly, it will tell people what you are up to and invite them to come and play in your sandbox so you can prosper together.

That is the **why** and the **what**. Here is the **how**.

Creating your vision

First pick a date. A vision is a present-tense description of a future date. Anything between six months and five years away is fine. I like a year or so. Then use these tools to release your creativity and structure your vision. Create more possibilities than you can realize—then, once you have done so, prune them and use what you have discovered to write a couple of paragraphs. It does not have to be Hemingway-quality—just blast it out the first time and tweak it later.

Put your heart into it. If life's got you down right now, picture what wonderful would look like. It may not magically appear under your Christmas tree, but I guarantee you this: if you have a picture of what awesome looks like, you are much more likely to achieve it, even if your circumstances and your starting place are constrained.

Here are the vision tools. Use two—or, for fun, do them all!

1) **Make a list of fifty things you would like to *be*, fifty things you would like to *do*, and fifty things you would like to *have*.** Yes, fifty. Each. That is the creative process, because the first ten will be same-old, same-old. Real novelty comes in once you get stuck and push through to fifty. You cross them off later.

BE	DO	HAVE
Productive	Attend a writer's workshop	A NYT best-seller
Kind	Do a 1 day Vipassana retreat	Several published e-books
Centered	Take Conor and Luca to Japan	A prosperous writing career
Great dad	Climb a 14er	A visiting faculty appointment
Hard-working	Win a WSOP bracelet	$25k in savings
Playful	Spend six weeks a year in London	Top ten leadership blog
Fun	Lots of dating	10,000 followers
Funny	Write a book on ADD/ Recovery	A Jaguar
Admired	Do a 2 day Vipassana retreat	A great MNC client
Prosperous	Do longer Vipassana retreats	$200k in annual income
Green (er)	Hit Harbin for writing/ reflection/ holiday	A nice, but simple house
Slim	Build the Science and Leadeship meme	A flat in Vegas/ London
Fit	Build the 21st Century Leadership meme	Reputation as visionary thinker
Present (kids)	Find a service position	Fantastic girlfriend
Compassionate	Contribute to important charities	Debt-free
Visionary	Speak 'on the circuit'	$50k Poker bankroll
Transformative	More nightclubbing	A Harley
Choiceful	Write a sci-fi novel	Conor/ Luca attend great college
Connected	Visit Asia/ India/ Middle East more	Happy, clever, self-expressed boys
Good son/ sibling	Take a Uni course with Conor	An NED position

Tip: Your "HAVEs" need not be selfish or materialistic. For example: "my school district is the best funded in the county," or, "my kid gets selected for the state swim team."

2) **Make a reverse timeline.** First pick areas that matter to you—health, wealth, family, career, etc. There should be seven to ten of those. Put those on the long side of a piece of paper. Now put some dates on the short side. Start

twenty-five years out. Then ten, then five, four, three, two, and one. Now write what you want to see. In 1994, I did this with a friend and we said, "We want to have our own business by 2005" (we were working for "the man" at the time). We then wrote down where we would need to be in the intervening years—we would need skills, qualifications, experience, followers, capital, and connections. Well we wrote it down, and then we did it. A step at a time. I grew the business to $4 million in value by 2008, and though it was battered by the recession, I eventually sold it for $1 million.

Tip: The columns matter a lot. Use your day one "areas of life". People serious about career need both a career and a job category.

Year-end	Writing	Brand/ platform	Teaching/ Speaking	Finance	Hobbies	Health	Kids	Relationships
2040	Twenty books/ five transformative one's							
2030	Major literary award							
2025	Ten books/ three transformative						Luca college, Conor starts work	
2020	One NYT best-seller			Prosperous 2030 plan	Win WSOP or major event		Conor college/ Luca HS	
2016	Start novel/ one more NF		Permanent research faculty appt'	Buy house	Win major event, run 2x mini tris			
2015	21st Century Leadership book	Top ten 'leading thinkers on business', big demand as advisor	12 speaking gigs	$25k savings/ $25k roll	Buy Harley or Jag, win major event		Luca KG/ Con MS - terrific summer vacation	
2014	WCF finished, 3 e-books finished	Top ten leadership blog	Adjunct Prof/ Six speaking gigs/ 10 days teaching	$150,000 income/ debt free by year-end/ everything complete	Do first mini-triathlon, super profitable series	88 kilos/ pass major checkup/ normal lipids	Transform kids diet/ lifestyle	Lots and lots of dating/ time with close friends
2013	Agent/ publisher WCF, One e-book published	1000 followers, world class site		$50,000 advance		98 kilos year end	House is yell-free zone	Ready to date, rebuild friendships

3) **Draw a picture** If you can't draw, grab a ton of magazines and make like a kindergartener with glue sticks and scissors. Get a big piece of brown paper and start designing your future visually. I did this with my partner (business partner and wife) before we launched our lives together in 2001. It all

happened. The dreams came true: we created and ran a business for eight years, traveled the world, made a difference to thousands of lives, and created a beautiful family. [1].

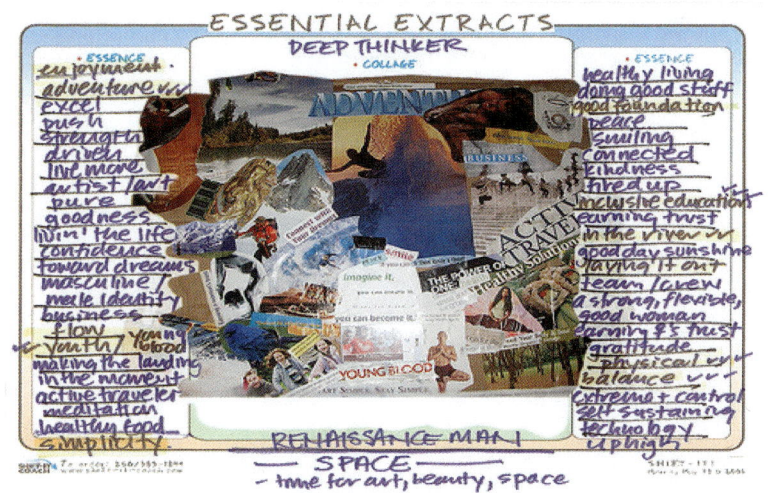

4) **Have an imaginary reunion with a friend**. It is 2020. You bump into a friend you have not seen since 2010. They say, "Hey, let's have a cup of coffee and why don't you tell me what's up?" So you tell them all about how 2020 looks—what you are doing, what you have achieved, and what is on the horizon. Details matter. The way to do this is to actually imagine the conversation and jot down notes, perhaps using a mind map, of the things you would say.

Here is what a finished one might look like:

My writing career kicked off in 2013 with an e-book

---

[1] *Collage reproduced with permission from SHIFT-IT-Coach Inc. and Christina Merkley.*

and a popular website/blog. In 2014, my first full-length business book, The Science of Organizational Change, *was published, and the writing and publicity process brought in writing, speaking and teaching opportunities. I touch lives and make them better with practical tools. The science and leadership/21st-century leader meme has caught hold, and I am the go-to guy. I've got a portfolio of well-paying clients, and am in greater demand on the speaking circuit. My website sales, traffic, and campaigns generate enough for living expenses and my consulting income generates surplus.*

I am raising two superb young men. Luca is starting kindergarten and Conor junior high, and I work hard to make the time spent with them rich and high-quality. I'm starting to show them around the world, and I spend my free travel time taking them to fun places. I'm a super-healthy fifty-five. I did my first mini-triathlon in 2014, and I do one a year now. The spread I had at fifty has diminished, and while I'm not twiggy, you can at least see where the six-pack belongs. I keep in touch with close friends around the world, have local friendships, and have a great woman in my life.

Day 8 – Setting inspiring goals

Goals work their "magic" in our subconscious, focusing our attention and helping our mind sift through choices that we face daily.

—Paul Gibbons

How goal-setting works

When you set a goal or intention, you tell your mind to pay attention to different things. Scientists have estimated the amount of data (images, sounds, sensations) that arrives to meet us each day, and it is vast (measured in Exabytes). If you processed all the visual and auditory information that came your way, you would be disoriented and perhaps a little nuts. So we have trained ourselves to focus on some things and avoid others. Who could remember the tune of the Muzak playing in the department store? Yet you will remember the song the bride and groom chose for their first dance at a wedding because you paid attention to it.

It works like this: Say you have never gone on a Caribbean cruise, but in a creative space like this one, you decide it would be an once-in-a-lifetime pleasure and set a distant goal. I seldom notice all the glossy ads in magazines that I read, do you? I skim quickly to the good stuff. But having set a goal like that, a picture of a boat sailing next to sandy beaches and palm trees might get your attention. And you might do something about that—make a call, clip the ad, open that savings account, or something else that brings it closer to you.

If you have the business goal of doubling the size of your network and deepening relationships within it, you will receive the deluge of inputs from social media differently. (Perhaps I should attend that conference, or join that networking group, or connect via social media?)

If you set the goal of "being more assertive as a leader" but shrink from that in a key meeting, the dissonance between the goal and your behavior will reach your attention. You can then resolve to do some specific things differently next time.

Goal-setting works like magic, but it is not magic. It requires setting an intention, creating some practices or strategies for getting there, honestly monitoring your progress, and having the courage to self-correct along the way.

Setting your goals

Now we are going to set one to four goals for each "domain of success" we created on Day 1. We are also going to set some measures, where we can, so you will know when you have achieved a given goal.

As a reminder, sometimes measures can be results-oriented ("I will weigh 190 pounds by June 30th," or "I will increase my personal sales by 15 percent"), and sometimes measures can be process-oriented ("I will meet my financial advisor once in January and once in July to review," or "I will meditate five times a week for 15 minutes.")

Here is an example of what the goal-setting template looks like when completed. I have only included three domains of success. You will see that in health/well-being, I have a target but also (more importantly) weekly goals for getting me there. The rightmost column will be used when you review your progress on a monthly basis (or so), either to nudge yourself back on track or to celebrate as goals are reached:

Goals to May 2014	Measure	Status	30-Nov	31-Dec	31-Jan
Career/ branding					
- Top 50 leadership blog	- site up to 100 hits a day by Dec				
- Secure local TEDx	or equiv				
- Secure IAAP talk	or equiv				
- LinkedIn influencer	or equiv				
- IEE talk	or equiv				
Teaching/ webinars/ blog					
- convert local ops - Jim LoP and Jim F					
- first webinar online and generating income	Jan start, by March 31st				
- first Youtube video published	Jan start, by March 31st				
- productive blogger	- 2 guest posts per month/ 10 Daily P/ 4 Lead Yourself				
- Site 2.0 (ecommerce and SEO)	- April start				
Writing					
- Reboot published and sell 5000 copies	publish end Nov/ 5000 by May				
- Reboot repurposed for ADD/ Divorce/ Poker	publish end March				
- Why Change Fails draft completed	Ch 3 Nov, 4 Dec, etc		Ch 3	Ch 4	Ch 5
- WCF publisher found	by Jan 31				
- WCF agent found					
Health/ well-being					
- regular practices	- 3x cross-fit type intensity/ 2x 30m light workout				
- lose 8 kg to 96kg	- myNetDiary in use				
- change health insurance	- by Jan 1st				
- get teeth cleaned/ lipids/ prostate checked	- by May				
- regular meditation/ yoga	- 10m per day start up to 30m per day by May				

Different kinds of goals

Before launching into goal-creating, there are a few distinctions in the goal-setting area that are essential to creating and achieving big ones:

Performance goals versus learning goals

Great leaders (including in the area of "leading yourself") do not just focus on achievement, they also focus on expanding their ability to contribute and achieve. Steven Covey calls this "sharpening the saw," but the metaphor can be extended to "learning how to saw more efficiently." Michael Jordan, even at the peak of his abilities, used to review his games thoroughly—to look for "leaks." Ask yourself the question, in key areas, "What could I learn that would yield the biggest improvements?"—and set a goal to learn it.

Stretch goals versus comfort zone

Goals should stretch you, but should be achievable. People differ: some play things super safe when setting goals, and some set goals that only Superman could achieve. In the exercise domain, there are structured ways to get from "couch potato" (someone perhaps exhausted after a 2-minute run) to a 5k run, but the process takes approximately half a year. Almost everyone can achieve something like this, but your goals need to reflect current reality (though not too much so!).

Results goals and process goals

In some areas, you want to focus on the process, not the result. For example, in the wellness domain, exercising five times a week is a process goal. In the workplace, holding a monthly coaching meeting with each of your staff is as well. Results goals will have a clear measure and a clear date by when they will be achieved. Process goals will have daily, weekly, or monthly targets. Process goals are critical because in some areas results only unfold over time—so the object is to develop great habits that deliver long-term and hard-to-measure value.

What to do now

Using the template in Appendix 1, create between one and four inspiring goals in each of your "domains of success". Recall what we have said about appropriate level of stretch, the difference between performance and leaning goals (and the importance of a mixture of those), and goals that focus on the result versus goals that focus on the means. After this process, most people have between 15 and 20 goals, but you might have more.

From Competence to Excellence

As with everything in life, there are levels of competence, excellence, and mastery. Now, 2/3 of the way through this process, most people are competent at leading the self-directed life. You have cleared away some debris, tallied where you are in important areas, established a foundation of integrity and gratitude, set the big picture for your life, and created some inspiring goals.

Days 9 and 10 represent the door to mastery, and subsequently they take some effort to learn and put into practice. If you lead a complex life, with multiple career and job commitments, and dozens of things that you manage and execute on a weekly basis (along with chores, errands, paying bills, and feeding kids), then mastering the process for days 9 and 10 will produce tremendous benefit.

Give them some earnest effort, but if after days 9 and 10, you feel you can realize your goals without their help, go for them with gusto. Depending on the life you lead, you may already have 80% of the value by now.

Day 9 – Turning goals into projects

Most people vastly overestimate what they can do in a day, and vastly underestimate what they can achieve in a decade.
—Adapted from Tony Robbins

Where we are now

We are now going to look at turning the goals you set in Day 8 into reality. It may feel as if we have generated a lot of complexity and a lot of lists. There is no question that this is true, but my promise to make your life *less* complex and stressful endures.

The stuff on the rug and runway lists was always there. The complexity of doing that exercise merely uncovered what was running around in your head, causing stress and costing focus, clarity, and concentration.

Still, you will be relieved to know that we are moving back toward simplicity now, with the goal of making it clear, every moment of every day, what you will be doing to realize your ambitions.

> **"Lean heavily on your someday-maybe list. It is your get out of jail free card if you are overwhelmed or stressed."**

One thing that helps with that "I'm overwhelmed by this" feeling at this stage is your "Someday-Maybe" list—your new best friend. For example, one executive I worked with, having created a list of fifty projects and a long rug/runway list of nearly one hundred items was exhausted just looking at it. My counsel was, "Relax and lean on your 'Someday-Maybe' list." There is only so much you can do in a day/week, and now that everything that has your attention is listed, you are in a position to make powerful choices rather than doing the first thing that jumps into view.

Even this simple prioritization—between things you are keen to move forward with during a day/week and things you care about that you are saying "no" to—can be of great benefit.

The following diagram provides an overview of where we have come from, where we are now, and where we are going.

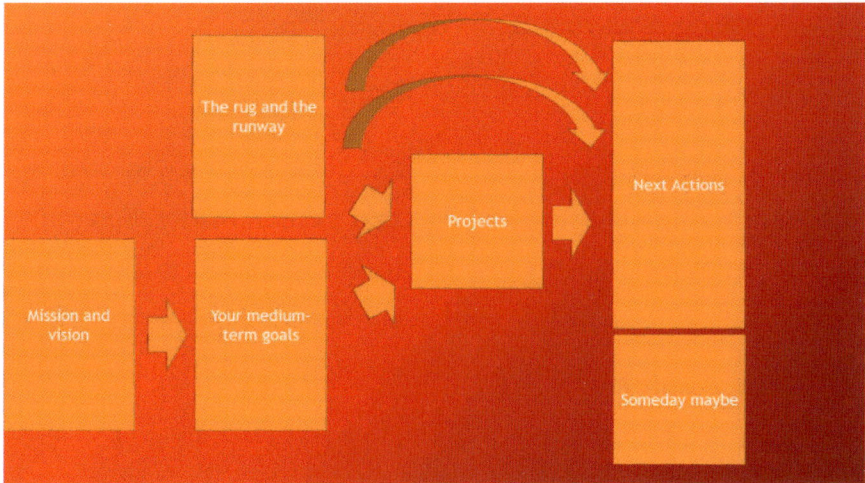

As you can see from the diagram, we are at the "beginning of the end." Today's mission is to turn your goals into projects. But why projects?

Huge results, little steps

There is an old saw that asks, "How do you eat an elephant?" The answer: "One bite at a time."

Okay, not funny, but there is a philosophical beauty in realizing that however big your goal is, it will *only* be accomplished through tiny tasks such as:

> ➢ Making a single phone call/writing a single email

- ➢ Writing a single paragraph (or word, even!) of that #**&@! report
- ➢ Convening a single meeting
- ➢ Researching a single topic
- ➢ Having a single critical conversation

If you imagine that your intentions and goals are the engine of a car and your hands are the wheels that provide the traction and results, today's work is the transmission that connects the engine to the wheels. Take all that engine energy (your goals) and translate those into "bites" you can do, right now, one at a time.

In our chaotic world, where everything seems to have to fit into 5 minutes or 140 characters, breaking things into small chunks may be the only way to stay sane.

How it works—a personal story

In 2008, I had a "pinch myself" moment. I was out of body, floating above a room, asking "Is this for real, or am I about to wake up?" I was in the boardroom of the biggest bank in the world—HSBC bank, which towers over London's skyline—and it was filled with twenty of my colleagues and one hundred HSBC executives, including the chairman and CEO. I was talking to the chairman of the biggest German bank, Deutsche Bank, about what we might do for him. Everyone there was gathered to review the last year of work that my company, Future Considerations, had done for them.

Seven years before, such a scenario was very unlikely. 80

percent of new businesses fail within two years, and my dream was formed with no capital, no staff, no clients, and in my living room in 2001. There are thousands of boutique consulting firms (not to mention huge ones, such as Harvard Executive Education) and tens of thousands of sole proprietor coaches angling for a piece of the most lucrative leadership development work. Though the market is competitive, I didn't wanna be one of those wannabes. I had a vision (that was all I had), of a leading-edge leadership development firm that would work with the top ten or twenty companies in the world and that would compete with Harvard and Stanford in the leadership development area—but it looked a long shot.

Late in 2000, I made the big choice to start my own company in 2001 rather than accept partnership at a huge consulting firm. When my new venture launched, I wanted to hit the ground running so I could earn money from the outset and not spend the first months filling out income tax forms, persuading my accounting software to work, and printing business cards. Creating a business takes some effort—you need staff, money, clients, computer systems, marketing materials, sales plans, budgets, and much more.

The problem was that I worked full-time, which in consulting means sixty hours a week. How was I going to start something meaningful in the spare time that I did not have? Breaking that "start a business" goal into projects and then into bite-sized tasks allowed me to develop that infrastructure while still in full-time employment.

In November 2000, I got cracking. My goal was a May 1st, 2001 launch, and I created some projects under the goal of starting my own company. Here are some of those projects:

- ➢ Invent a company name
- ➢ Set up legal structure
- ➢ Create a strategy and business plan
- ➢ Get finance set up—bank accounts/software
- ➢ Produce marketing materials
- ➢ Build a community—staff and associates
- ➢ Start a "sales funnel"
- ➢ Create a financial buffer through savings

What projects look like with other goals

A big goal should have several projects. For example, one important goal for me is to write a best-selling book on leadership. That goal has spawned over ten projects as it has evolved, but it started with just three: (1) Write a winning book proposal; (2) Build a website and mailing list; and (3) Develop a social media platform.

Here are a few more examples:

GOAL: Make a big career change

Project 1: Do the "inner work" to get clearer about what a great new job would look like. (You might read a book or get some coaching.)

Project 2: Research companies and opportunities in your area.

Project 3: Craft a great resume.

Project 4: Network and increase social media exposure.

Project 5: Begin a campaign of contacting headhunters and firms.

GOAL: Lose weight/improve fitness

Project 1: Get clear on motivations, barriers, and goals. Work with coach/friend or write them down.

Project 2: Research and design incremental changes to diet. (Better than anything radical, which is unsustainable.)

Project 3: Research and obtain an Internet-tracking/motivation site.

Project 4: Get a personal trainer or exercise buddy.

Project 5: Start a sport/fun fitness activity (tennis, hiking, golf, etc.).

GOAL: Take a two-week 10th anniversary cruise (in 2 years)

Project 1: Research options and create "dream scenario."

Project 2: Get rough costs and create a special savings account.

Project 3: Find extra finances by selling unused household stuff.

Project 4: Get certified as scuba diver.

Project 5: Secure one freelance job per quarter to finance cruise.

Many big goals fail because of lack of a clear strategy for achieving them. These projects comprise your strategy, and as you can see, they allow you to tackle your goal from numerous perspectives. Consider how much more powerful the "fitness" goal is above when you have five different projects aimed at achieving it rather than just a vague "lose 10 pounds" goal.

What you need to do now

We have already identified a number of projects—those to do with clearing the rug and the runway. Now we are going to make a complete list of all your projects, including those we created earlier, and add those based on your goals.

You have your goals from Day 8. Using the "Goals to Projects" template in the Appendix, use your creativity to create projects that will make the goal real. If you struggle with this, ask a friend for help.

Create projects with inspiring titles. Do not worry if you don't feel you can do this exhaustively now. My "Write a bestseller" goal spawns new projects and grows each week. Many of the projects I now have on my list—for example, search engine optimization of my website—were not foreseen when I began.

When you have finished this, you will have a list of thirty to fifty projects (perhaps more). Next, we are going to break each one into baby steps, and you can choose which of those you will pursue based on your schedule and other commitments.

Day 10 – Turning projects into next actions

Why to-do lists fail

If you are like I was before I learned some of these methods, you write very long lists of things to do each day. On a great day, you complete a quarter or half of them. Humans have a cognitive bias (a hardware error) that makes us overestimate what we can do in a day. We fall short.

I used to find falling short every day de-motivating. Even on a day on which I was massively productive, I would still have a long, long list of stuff to do in my briefcase. The list followed me home, and I rarely had the sense of accomplishment and achievement that my efforts merited.

Another problem was that my list was hard to use. It was part "rug clearing," part "runway," part "goals," part "projects," and part "next actions." Hence it was a mixture of huge things (projects, goals, and dreams), and miniscule things (such as buying milk on the way home). Few goals and projects were boiled-down, crisp tasks such as "Call Jack" or "Discuss project risk with Diane." With many items, I had to figure out "what needs to happen now" as I worked through the list, which is a pain when you are feeling action-oriented.

I often prioritized the list, but it was so long that doing it was a chore. Furthermore, what was a priority action after my second cup of coffee at 8 AM, when I was full of energy, was an unrealistic priority at 6 PM, when I felt like a zombie.

Today, we are going to look at a different way of capturing actions into "Next Action" lists, lists that are a huge improvement upon standard to-do lists and that release a huge amount of energy and productivity.

> *"Lack of clarity on what to do next is the chief source*
> *of procrastination and resignation." (David Allen)*

From projects to next actions

Even though creating projects is a massive improvement in productivity for most people, you cannot *do* a project, you can only take an action. A personal project without a "next action" creates a world of pain. Take a project of "Complete last year's taxes," for example. That fills most people with dread, because their affairs might be messy, the outcome may be bad, or they be uncomfortable with numbers and forms. Not knowing where to begin (and hating it all to boot), they procrastinate. As time goes on, guilt and stress rise and deadlines may loom, creating a sense of resignation. Resignation leads to more procrastination. "Hello, this is the IRS calling about your tax return for . . ."

The power of next-action thinking is immense. David Allen, again the go-to guy on this aspect of self-management, illustrates the power of next-action thinking with the following coaching example: His client had "Tires" on his mindsweep. "What is that?" asked David. "I need new tires." "What is the next action?" David probed. "I need to call and make an appointment." "Do you have the number?" "No, my friend John recommended a good place, but I forgot the name." "So you need to call John? Do you have John's number?"

The next action, then, is: "Call John for name and number of tire place."

Perhaps you can see that what was a vague "yuck" ("Tires") turned into a quick, 30-second speed-dial to a friend. The same is true for taxes—the first action might be "Pull box full of receipts out of attic" or "Pay teenage son $25 to sort receipts into months and categories."

From projects to next actions—a personal story

To pick up my personal story from 2001—after I had created projects that would lead to a fast launch of my company, I still needed to accomplish them despite working sixty hours a week. If I had a half-hour lunch break, I needed something half-hour-sized to do. So I started "eating the elephant" in tiny bites, breaking those projects into tiny tasks. A nibble-sized week might look like:

➢ Call two friends for recommendations for logo/business card designers (20 mins.)
➢ Choose a designer based on recommendations (10 mins.)
➢ Brief designer (60 mins.)
➢ Complete legal registration paperwork (60 mins.)

I got a name (Future Considerations) after a month of brainstorming, fretting, talking to people, and fretting some more (the fretting took most of the time). Then, slowly, I built a website, opened bank accounts, completed legal paperwork, and talked to tax people. I also had one hundred meetings with potential clients and associates.

Despite having just a few hours each week, (and, as advertised in the introduction, being the most naturally disorganized businessperson you have ever met) I was ready to quit my job by mid-February. On Friday I walked out, and on Monday, February 19th I was the founder of my own consulting firm. My six-month project had taken less than four months—one bite at a time. More importantly than that, I had momentum on my side. That momentum provided me with my first household name client, British Airways, within a week, and my company, Future Considerations, grew at 60 percent a year until I sold out in 2009. It still prospers today.

Now take each of your projects and distill them down to bite-sized nibbles. Use the "Projects to Next Actions" template in the Appendix (or our Excel workbook). It is fine if each project, as you brainstorm next actions, generates lots of next actions—just jot those down next to the project, but make sure there is only one in the "Next Action" column.

Those next actions should be added to the quick-action list from Day 4 (when you cleared the rug and the runway) to create one single list of actionable next actions.

Making "Next Action" lists more useful

Now that you have a long "Next Action" list, there is a further step—making that list user-friendly so that you look forward to consulting it rather than shudder at the thought of it.

The way the list becomes user-friendly is when it only offers you the choices you can act upon. There are different ways to tackle this, and they depend on your lifestyle, ways of working, and type of job.

Option 1: Context-specific lists

David Allen suggests context-specific action lists. There are some actions you can only do at your computer, others when you just have a phone, others when you are driving around in your car, and yet others when you are at the office. When you have a lifestyle that gives you 30 minutes to kill at the airport, it is great to have a context-specific list called "Calls" so you can check off five or six of those. If those calls are mixed in with potential actions from fifty different projects, you will have to do a great deal of scanning, and if you are tired, that may be more effort than you feel like expending.

Another example is an "Errands" category of next actions: the things you can do when out and about for an hour. If you manage or work closely with people, you can have an "Agenda" for each of them where you list tasks you must accomplish with them—for example, "Assess project risk," "Delegate client report," "Follow up on last coaching session." Every time you meet you will be clear on what must be accomplished, which makes for very efficient meetings! Perhaps much of your work takes place in meetings? You can have a list to remind you of critical actions for you at the meeting: "Raise supply chain issue" or "Follow up on office move," for instance.

Here is a starter list, and I suggest you start with it if you choose this method (but first consider a second method, the one I use).

Basic action lists	
OFFICE/ COMPUTER (at-desk tasks)	HOME OFFICE (maybe home finances or burnishing your resume)
PHONE (things you can do with just a phone)	AGENDAS (you have key people you hold conversations with, such as "Review project progress with Jane")
ERRANDS	MEETINGS (you may have an action to raise an issue or propose something at a regular meeting)
HOME PROJECTS	READ/ REVIEW LIST

Option 2: Other next-action sorting methods

I don't use context-specific lists because (at the moment) I spend 95 percent of my productive time at my computer writing. Context-specific lists are terrific for people on the go, for road warriors, or for people who have lots of meetings and relationships and projects to manage (many office workers), but they work less well for me.

I prefer my lists sorted by activity. The way I manage my week is by setting big priorities (which we'll talk about tomorrow) and then allocating big blocks of time to get them done. If I have a few hours set aside for "blogging," I want to know which blogs I'm writing, reviewing, and guest posting on. I don't want to see "Take shirts to dry cleaner" or "Finish introduction to Chapter 3" on that list.

If you are (say) a designer or contractor of some kind who has multiple client projects on the go, you may want to block out time for a client and have a list of next actions for that client.

I also like to make a list called "Things I can do that will take under 5 minutes." If my productivity sags and I cannot bear to write another word, but feel I ought to keep working, it is useful to whip out a list of things I can accomplish in that brain-dead state.

My "list of lists" look like this:

Basic action lists	
BLOGGING	WRITING PROJECT A
WRITING PROJECT B	PERSONAL ADMIN
ERRANDS	QUICK TASKS
CALLS	RESEARCH/ READING

The upshot of this is that you have to make a choice of how to organize your "Next Action" lists. The truth is, you will not get this 100 percent right the first time, but you will eventually create a method that is perfectly personalized to the way you work.

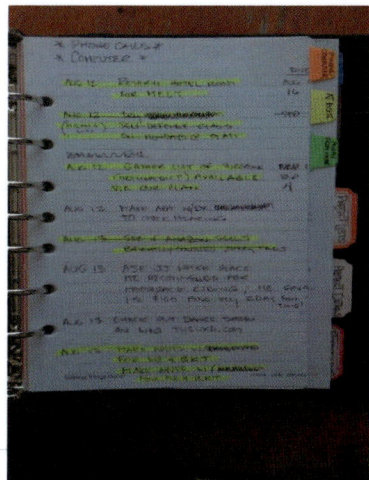

The task to complete today,

then, is to transfer your actions (or sort them, or cut and paste them) into categories that work for you. I reiterate that you should treat your new system as experimental and be prepared to tweak it to make it work better.

Using technology (or not)

Let us briefly revisit the three technological options for keeping up your system because now is the time to choose what you will implement for at least the next three months Paper, Evernote, and Excel. Here are some advantages and disadvantages to each.

Paper

One of my friends, an expert in this kind of self-management, had a plastic folder with twelve dividers for each of his lists. At the back of his folder he had Master Lists (such as projects and goals), and each of his "Next Action" categories had a divider devoted to it. Inside each division was a handwritten list of next actions. It was an extremely workable system. When he was in a meeting with "John," he could pop open his folder to his "John" list for things he needed to get done with John. When running errands, he could rip out the errand list and get on with it. In an airport, he always knew whom he needed to call when he had 20 minutes to spare.

He was a technophobic Luddite, but a highly effective one! You could use that method and never touch a keyboard.

Evernote

Evernote has a folder system and is accessible on your phone, laptop, PC, Mac, or tablet. I recommend it. It is the best personal organization software on the market, it is free, there are hundreds of articles on how to use Evernote

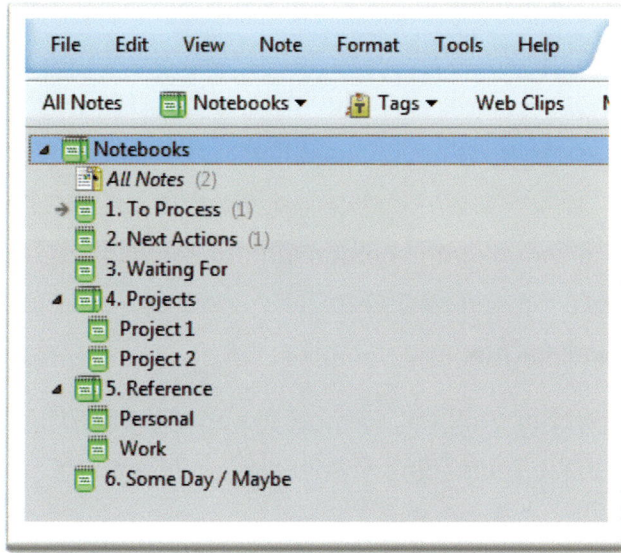

| File | Edit | View | Note | Format | Tools | Help |

All Notes   Notebooks ▼   Tags ▼   Web Clips

- ▲ Notebooks
  - *All Notes* (2)
  - → 1. To Process (1)
  - 2. Next Actions (1)
  - 3. Waiting For
  - ▲ 4. Projects
    - Project 1
    - Project 2
  - ▲ 5. Reference
    - Personal
    - Work
  - 6. Some Day / Maybe

with personal effectiveness routines, and (did I mention this?) it is free. Unless you are completely allergic to technology, use Evernote. It takes 5 minutes to install, and you can be using it in an instant.

Evernote is also an extremely potent anti-distraction tool! I spend hours researching on the Internet, and, like a magpie, am attracted to all the shiny things I find there. Evernote has a "clipper" that attaches to your browser so when you run into that great recipe for homemade dim sum while you are researching something else, with one click you can "clip" it to Evernote (or perhaps to your "Someday-Maybe" folder) to look at when the time is right and get back to what you were (ostensibly) focused on.

Excel

I use Excel because of the power of its sort, cut and paste, and color scheming. Evernote experts will complain that Evernote is just as powerful in those regards, and that if I were to bother to work a bit with it, it would do all Excel does and more. They are probably right. (Perhaps there are paper Luddites, and Microsoft Luddites too?!) I keep one "Next Action" list, but can quickly sort by the categories that matter to me with the click of a button, and I can cut and paste lists freely from one area to another—it works well for me.

Here is a snip of some of the tabs in the Excel workbook that I use for managing my own commitments.

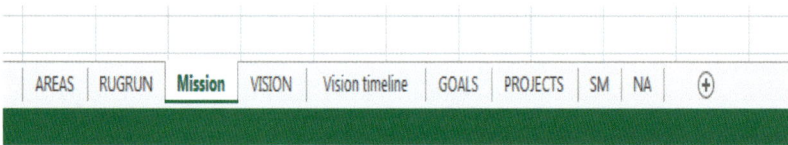

AREAS	RUGRUN	Mission	VISION	Vision timeline	GOALS	PROJECTS	SM	NA	⊕

Completing today

If you have worked hard through this process (and the last two days were very hard), you now have a really high-tech personal organizing system, one that is better than what 99 percent of the executives with whom I come into contact have. It is based around your mission, vision, and goals, which you've developed into projects, and your next actions are sorted in a way in which you can quickly access and accomplish them.

If you are used to working off a single to-do list, this may seem cumbersome at first, but I invite you to give it a whirl. You can

always revert to a single next-action list after a few weeks of
trying something new.

Your lists are now:

➢ Action lists (perhaps context specific, or perhaps grouped into
  projects/ clients) that are quick and easy to find, and which
  offer you only the choices that make sense given what you are
  up to or what resources you have available
➢ A Someday-Maybe list where you put parked items, but which
  you review frequently
➢ A projects list (that you will use to create new actions when
  you check things off)
➢ A list of goals (which you will update as you finish projects or
  realize goals)
➢ Long-term lists, such as mission and vision statements, which
  you will revise perhaps annually

Our last two days will focus on two practices: the weekly "self-
leadership" practice of allocating time to that which is most
important, and, finally, keeping your system fresh and vital so it
continues to work for you.

Day 11 – Deciding what to do when

I learned that we can do anything, but we can't do everything . . . at least not at the same time. So think of your priorities not in terms of what activities you do, but when you do them. Timing is everything.

—Dan Millman

The highest-leverage thing that you can do—the one that gives you the most bang for your buck each week—is to plan your week by referring to your "Goals," "Projects," and "Next Action" lists. I worked with a CEO of a 400 million-dollar business who entered each week without a single free moment for planning, strategy, coaching, or reflection. His assistant managed his calendar, and by the time he saw it, there was no space. People lower down in organizations constantly feel as if very little of their time is theirs to command, but ahhh, were they higher up the pecking order, their time problems would disappear. No—time problems multiply.

Getting control of your calendar is the essence of productivity. It sounds trivial to say, but time is your most valuable and precious resource. 30 minutes spent thinking about how you will invest this time on a weekly (and daily) basis is critical. Do the math. 30 minutes to think about how you use the (roughly) 4,320 productive minutes in a week. Invest 30 to get greater yield from the other 4,290!

Prioritizing in action

Steven Covey made a beautiful distinction between **importance** and **urgency**, one that had life-changing effects when I began to use it twenty years ago. Urgency is the incoming stuff that looks as if it cannot wait—emails, phone calls, deadlines, and meetings. Urgency is not all bad; some urgent things might be finishing a project you have been working on for a year, or planning your 20th wedding anniversary. Those tasks (projects) are urgent *and* important.

But neither is urgency all good. If you get caught doing only the urgent, your ability to create long-term value is diminished. The urgent screams at us; the important whispers quietly.

As leaders grow in accountability in their careers, they must increasingly lift their gaze from the day-to-day and focus on delivering long-term value and building long-term capability. You cannot do that when stuck in urgency mode.

Important stuff, by contrast, adds **long-term value** to your life, to your vision, and to the lives of people around you. Most e-mails do not do that.

The at-risk stuff is **important** but not **urgent**. Booking a seminar to acquire a key skill, taking time out to coach a struggling co-worker (or your kid), taking an hour to reflect creatively on strategy for a new project, spending time nurturing a relationship, and exercising are important but not terribly urgent. Mostly, nobody will notice if you fail to do the things in the important, non-urgent category—and you might not either, unless you have the practice of identifying what those things are for you.

Covey introduced a four-quadrant diagram, and for many years this was the only weekly time-management tool that I used. If you do nothing else on a weekly basis, looking at your commitments through this lens is transformative.

Here is an example of four-quadrant time-management in action. I took my task list and broke it out into the four quadrants:

Urgent, important	Not-urgent, important
Finish Chapter 12 Reboot	One hour on leadership blogs
Review manuscript	Schedule 3x cross-fit
Complete blog for Calleam	Meditate 5 x 10m
Complete landing page	Fix panels on site
Amazon seller account	Mind map Chapter 3!!!
Fix site sign-ups	Schedule 3x 30m workout
Edit Sue Blog	Prepare November budget
Complete cover briefing	
Urgent, not important	*Not-urgent, not-important*
Fix license	WSOP final table
Call water repair guy	**Some** social media time
Arrange accom Monday	
Pay Denver	
Clear inbox	

The top-left quadrant, **urgent and important**, is where the goodies are. This is where you deliver value to the world and yourself. You meet commitments, fulfill promises, attain goals, and forward the action in your big projects. The **urgent, not-important** stuff is stuff that cries out for your attention, but that does not add a great deal of long-term value to you or anybody else.

On a weekly basis, it is worth looking at your life through this lens. Pay special attention to the top-right, **important, not-urgent** quadrant. What projects and actions, given your long-term goals and priorities, risk getting swept away in the tsunami of urgency?

Scheduling important, not-urgent tasks

Schedule management is the second to last piece of our personal effectiveness puzzle. Most people I coach have had the experience of sitting down at their computer early in the morning with a few critical tasks to complete that day, but they "just check a few emails" first—and surface an hour or two later. When they do this, the effect on their mood is sometimes catastrophic. What started as a morning ripe with potential for creativity and productivity has turned into a mind-numbing distraction fest.

Add three, four, or five meetings and a half-dozen impromptu talks with colleagues to that sort of start, and you can easily arrive at 6 PM with the feeling that nothing has been done. Of course, plenty has been done, but all of it reactive, and none of it the few tasks you had deemed (with a clear head) critical.

It was in Covey that I first read the "big rocks" story, which is often told but worth reviewing.

A motivational time-management speaker brought out a large glass urn and asked a member of the audience to fill it to the top with large rocks. When finished, he asked whether it was full, and his assistant responded "yes." The speaker then topped it up with smaller rocks, which filled in the spaces between the big rocks. Asking again whether it was full, and gaining a further "yes," he added gravel. After asking again, he added sand, and after asking a last time, he added water.

"What does this have to do with time management?" he asked the audience.

"The big rocks would not have fit unless they were put in first."

In your life, most emails and distractions are the sand and the water. Fill your morning with those, and good luck finding time for big rocks. The big rocks have to go in first, but how do you do that?

You need to plan your week and put the big rocks in before competing commitments can grab the time.

Planning your week

At the beginning of your week, or when you create project task that will require protected time, you need to put that instantly in your calendar—before a meeting is scheduled, before a friend asks you to lunch, before you get swept up in email and web activity. For example, if you need to prepare for a meeting at which you are giving a presentation, schedule that. If you decide that your health, stress, and creativity will be serve by a 20-minute walk during lunch, schedule that. If you decide that you want two hours to creatively brainstorm your start-up idea with a friend, you schedule that. If you decide that your partner's birthday requires a few hours to choose a thoughtful present, you schedule that. Again, the most important things to schedule are those that are **important but not urgent**, because **urgent but not important** tasks will starve those of time if you let them.

Here is an example of scheduling with Covey's "Urgent, not Important" tasks colored in green:

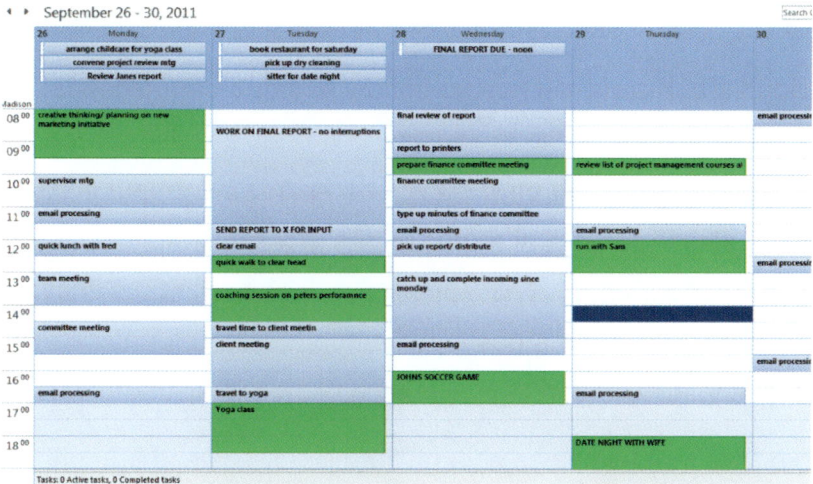

Those things you "should" do but never get time for, you either choose, schedule, and do, or drop that self-critical "should" from your vocabulary. That is loser/ victim talk. Yoda was right—there is no try, only do or not do.

Now look at your calendar of commitments for the coming weeks. Cast your eye over those really important tasks that you just know might not get done, and put those in with a fortress-like wall around them.

Many people struggle to do this because people are used to them saying yes instantly or being available to put out other's fires. During the first week, you may have to start small and not try to grab 40 hours where before you had no control over 40 minutes.

Using your calendar to decide what to do

Many highly effective people use the following technique for daily planning: There are two kinds of actions—time-sensitive ones (that occur at a specific time) and those that need to be done during the day sometime. The time-sensitive actions—a meeting or the (important, not-urgent) preparation for a meeting must be done at a specific time.

Next actions that must be done on a specific day are put in the "all-day event" part of the calendar (at the top in Outlook and web-based calendar apps). That space is usually only occupied by random holidays from around the world and birthdays for people you barely know (if you let some apps put those in).

Make sure that you block enough time in your calendar to get to those big actions at the top of your calendar, or else you will find yourself attending to them when you could be with your spouse or kids or watching *Ice Road Truckers*.

The e-mail problem

If we could, without help, dedicate minutes to tasks that merit minutes, and hours to tasks that merit hours, we would have few problems. However, there is an apt saying: "Work expands to fill the time available." Give me 10 minutes to power through one hundred e-mails, and my responses will be tight, and all those wonderful, interesting articles from *People Magazine* will be properly deleted or parked. Give me an hour, however, and all links will be clicked and all my correspondents will get mini-novellas in response. If I'm facing a difficult problem, or something I wish to avoid, the problem gets worse.

Some businesses have silly expectations about response times to internal e-mails. While you might be (now) good at long-term thinking, the urgency addicts are still running around fighting fires and expecting you to show up with the hose at the drop of a hat.

You need to slowly extricate yourself from that game.

One leader shared during a workshop that her boss had a habit of storming around the corner 10 minutes after sending an e-mail if he had not received a response. (One wonders why, if it were urgent, he did not pop around the corner in the first place.) Such situations are tricky to handle but must be handled. Most bosses will be amenable to the argument that you are trying to improve personal productivity by doing e-mail only at specific intervals. Ask if there is another way very urgent requests can be delivered.

E-mail best practice is to allocate a fixed, reasonably short space of time to attend to them at periods during the day. Early morning, noon, and before leaving are typically such times.

The trick for getting through one hundred e-mails in a short period is to triage them. Ruthlessly file or delete all non-essential ones. Quickly attend to those that require one-minute responses: "Thanks for this, looking forward to see you in two weeks." Those that require more thoughtful responses can be handled during that period, but if you're out of time, **schedule a time to thoughtfully respond, either during that day or appropriately soon.**

In this manner, you can remain strict about your 30-minute e-mail windows and get back to high-priority, important tasks.

Further e-mail tips:

1) **Turn off all e-mail reminders.** Most e-mail programs have multiple ways of alerting you to an incoming e-mail. I am ADD-prone, so such flickers or sounds are toxic to my productivity. I snap-click, open my inbox, and (of course) there are twenty new e-mails "demanding" attention, and 30

minutes disappear into the ether. Turn all of those off.

2) **Your email inbox is NOT your to-do list.** You need to schedule e-mail and use it, rather than it scheduling you and using you! Sure you may discover something during your 30-minute e-mail trawls that just can't wait, but ask yourself first whether that is really true. If it is true, then do it, but beware of the urgency of that e-mail conflicting with the importance of other commitments. You are not just saying "yes" to attending to that e-mail, you are saying no to a bunch of other (important) things.

3) **The more you send, the more you receive.** The ratio is approximately 2.5 received per one sent. If you want to receive fewer emails, send fewer emails. Beware CC and BCC, and use those only when absolutely necessary. Consider this: an email sent to ten people, each of whom "reply-all," which elicits yet a further "reply-all" from each, generates one thousand emails.

Day 12 – Keep this going—for the rest of your life

If you get to this page having done the work on the previous eleven days, then congratulations! The changes you're making, even if they seem small, over a year or a decade can be huge. Say you invent one new practice of starting your day with 15 minutes of exercise and 15 minutes of personal planning. The former makes you more focused, lowers your stress, and gains you some impulse control. The latter means you are always working on the right stuff. The graph of your life (success, fulfillment, achievement, flow) nudges higher each day.

Incremental improvements, whether in time management, focus, pursuing goals, building relationships, adding skills, or developing yourself, add up *geometrically* over time. For example, if you improve at something by 5 percent per week, how much better are you after thirteen weeks (a financial quarter)? Nearly twice as good!

What we have accomplished during the last eleven days is to set a foundation for you improving incrementally—being 5 percent more productive, paying 5 percent more attention to *your* goals, or dedicating 5 percent more time to your future and the relationships you care most about.

In a quarter, you will be astonished!

This process may also yield a radical transformation. You may have set out on a new path, a new goal, a new job, or a new commitment to a neglected area. In that case, your "life-graph" may veer sharply higher rather than just nudging higher.

Our job now is to make sure that our twelve days together continue to help you grow and achieve. That requires two things of you: your commitment to continually rejuvenate this process, and your getting support for your big goals.

Rejuvenating our process

One thing we have done is clear your head by making some lists (such as the "Someday-Maybe" list) of things that you do not want to forget but do not want to worry about currently. You have also done some personal planning, goal-setting, and housekeeping. You may be clearer about your commitments, and what to say yes and no to, than ever before.

Life is going to keep coming at you, and you must have a way of keeping this process alive. Here's how you do that:

Weekly:

> ➢ Do a mindsweep (Day 3) and decide which items will get your attention that week (Day 4).
> ➢ Review your list of projects and design next steps for all of them (Day 9).
> ➢ Review your upcoming schedule (calendar) and put the big rocks in (Day 11).

Monthly:

> ➢ In addition to the weekly items, review your "Someday-Maybe" lists and your goal lists (Day 8).

> ➢ Use those to update your projects and "Next Action" lists (Days 9 and 10).

Annually:

> ➢ Decide now when you are going to redo this process in the coming year (perhaps twelve months from now, or perhaps at year-end).
>
> ➢ Set aside perhaps four or five hours over a two-week period for this process. It is much faster each time you do it, and if you have be on the ball monthly, the whole annual review may take but a few hours.

On being a beginner

And now a word on relapse. Gravity never takes a day off. You will, I guarantee, fall short of your ideals (otherwise they are not high enough). The difference between people who achieve greatness through personal change and those who don't is precisely one thing: how well they fail.

Put another way, failure is not falling down, it is staying down.

Most gym memberships are disused after January 31st. This is because the "I'm going to go six times a week" resolution, earnestly made, is unsustainable for someone who has spent the past eleven months on the couch. And the first time that person misses an appointment, they say "There I go again, I'm a piece of &*%# and will never get this right." Does that make them *more* or *less* likely to go the next day? They fall into a spiral of one broken promise, guilt, resignation, more broken promises.

You are probably a beginner at this type of process, and although it seems simple, living a goal-driven life takes some skill and practice. The first time you do anything, it should feel clunky. You will also fail—you will forget to check in weekly, or your calendar may get out of control, or you may find yourself back in the rut you temporarily lifted yourself out of.

Get used to it. Nobody does this perfectly.

Now—what will you do when you fail? Will you get back on the horse? How? What will you say to yourself? What do you want others (and who are they?) to say to you? Be specific.

Getting support

Aristotle thought a true friend was not just someone with whom you socialize, but someone who is prepared to get in your face. You need someone like that alongside you during this process. Your Day 12 assignment is to find that person and spend 30 minutes taking them through what you have done. You want to make them your "committed listener." A committed listener is someone who cares about you but doesn't put up with your "stuff" and excuses. Sure, you gossip, watch TV, play golf, and chill with them—but you must change gears also for this bit to work. Create a space in your relationship where you aren't buddies or girlfriends or husband and wife but where they are there listening to your greatness *and* they have permission to kick your tail.

The promises

If you have been painstaking about going through this process, you will feel a new aliveness and passion now. You will feel your life is on track, even though it may not be where you want it to be at the moment. Everybody has down days, but when you have one, you can lift your gaze to the horizon and focus on the road ahead.

Thank you for allowing me to join you virtually on this journey. As my Irish ancestors said: "May the road rise to meet you, may the wind be always at your back, and may you be in Heaven an hour before the Devil knows you are dead."

About Paul Gibbons

Paul Gibbons has thirty years' business experience in banking, consulting, and academia. While based in Europe, he worked with senior leadership of the world's most respected companies to help them deliver strategy through leadership development and culture change. He began his career at Credit Suisse First Boston, then moved to PricewaterhouseCoopers, first as an expert on strategy and risk management, then as a member of PwC's global Innovation Think Tank, and finally as a leader in their culture change practice.

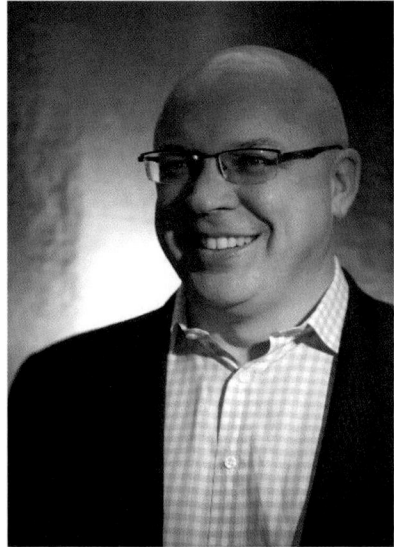

In 2001, he founded his own consulting firm, which grew at 60 percent a year until he sold the business in 2009. That firm, Future Considerations, worked with five of the top ten UK companies on leadership, culture, and sustainability issues, and won Europe-wide recognition for the results that it produced for those clients, including Shell, BP, HSBC, Barclays, Cadbury, and KPMG.

Paul is qualified as a Master Coach, and in 2006 he was written up in CEO magazine as one of two "CEO Super Coaches." His writing and teaching focus on the application of neuroscience, behavioral economics, and philosophy to create business breakthroughs. He holds degrees in neurochemistry, organizational psychology, and philosophy, and has held teaching positions at a number of European and US universities. He lives in Fort Collins, Colorado, with his two sons, Conor and Luca.

Acknowledgments

I'd first like to honor Steven Covey's great work *The Seven Habits of Highly Effective People*, which I first read in 1994 and I think is the best book ever written on personal development. A few years later, I recruited Laura Finestone as a coach, and her great questions helped unleash a ton of productivity and creativity over the coming decade. Ed Lamont, a successful London coach and entrepreneur who lives and breathes this kind of process, helped me to see the value I had created and added some rigor to my goal-setting and practices. In 2006, my firm Future Considerations became David Allen's European partner. David's *Getting Things Done* takes Covey's personal effectiveness work to an entirely new level, and no contemporary author surpasses his authority in this area. My great client and friend Matthew Gregory produced a much-shortened version one year while I was sitting on my hands, and he encouraged me to formalize and structure this process so that others might benefit from it. I'd also like to thank all the reviewers, (especially the painstaking Megan Worthing-Davies), and all the hundreds of people on various social media sites who have responded to endless questions about titles, branding, content and the like.

Appendix 1 – Printable worksheets

Day 1 – Identifying your domains of success

First, using the instructions from Day 1, list the areas you have decided are important to you. (Seven to twelve is about right.) Be creative as well as descriptive. Second, rate your level of fulfillment on a scale of 1 to 10. Last, describe in one sentence what a "10" looks like.

Domains of success		
Area	Rating	What a "10" looks like
Example: Health	6	Lean, vital, energetic. Seeing my kids have kids.

Day 2 – What is under your rug?

Take 30 minutes and complete this exercise to your own satisfaction. Some prompts overlap. You don't need to repeat answers. The overlaps sometimes trigger different ideas, actions, and insights.

List any incomplete projects that you have stopped working on or no longer feel committed to:

> Tip: These are generally projects we would do at home, not at work, because at work we are held to account by people around us. Include house,

List any disaster areas—desk, home, garage, car, drawers, filing, and closets:

Tip: Opening that closet into which everything that does not have another place goes and seeing it full to the brim with you-know-not-what saps your energy.

List anything not complete around money:

Tip: Wills, investments, taxes, insurance, debts, and

List any persistent health issues you have been ignoring.

Tip: Check-ups, scans, diet, exercise, dentists, and

List your disappointments (coulda, woulda, shouldas) and unmet expectations of yourself.

Who are you resentful toward that you need to forgive? Who
resents you where you might have to ask forgiveness?

In what ways am I not living my purpose or my values? Which
ideals have I abandoned?

Tip: Some ideals need to be let go of, but let go of with peaceful acceptance. Some you will want to recommit to. Recommit to those that still serve you

Anything else you need to jot down that would lighten your load?

Day 3 – Your blank mindsweep template

This is an example of a mindsweep template from Coggle. Free mind mapping software can be obtained here: http://freemind.sourceforge.net/wiki/index.php/Download.

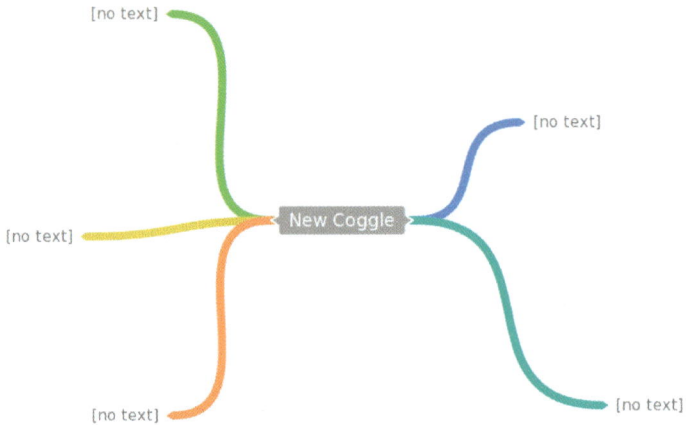

Day 4 – Clearing the rug and the runway

Once you have listed your items, simply make an "x" in the appropriate column to begin with. Start at the top, making quick decisions.

Once you have gone through the list, deciding where items should go, then create separate lists for each category: DUMP, SOMEDAY-MAYBE (DEFER), PROJECTS (PLAN), DO, and DELEGATE.

This is **much** easier in Excel or in Evernote because you can simply sort then cut and paste into a new workbook or note. The downloadable workbook I provide has tabs with those lists already prepared. If you do this in longhand, you will likely need 3 to 4 pages the first time, so you may have to photocopy the second page a few times.

Rug or runway item	DUMP	DEFER	PLAN	DO	DELE-GATE

Reboot Your Life

Day 5 – An attitude of gratitude

Using the instructions in the chapter dedicated to this day, complete this and make plans to call the people on it and tell them.

I am grateful for...	

Day 6 – Creating a personal mission

Answer the questions below, then begin crafting your two- to three-sentence mission statement.

What forces, people, and events have most influenced you and your passions? *(For example, my parents grew up poor but education saved them from a life of poverty, and I grew up surrounded by university professors; the importance of scholarship is in my DNA. Or, I grew up in family that struggled to make it financially, and, as a result, I always want my family to be secure.)*

What, looking back, have you always cared about? *(What sort of things interest you when nobody is looking? When you were young, what did you want to become?)*

What, again looking back, have been the ways in which you have spent your time? *(e.g., I have always had a profound love of reading, going back to very early age . . . this leads me to the idea that part of my mission is about books and great ideas.)*

When you reflect on it, what do you find that you are passionate about today? *(One way to discover this is to see what makes you angry. But transform that anger! If I'm angry about X, then I must care deeply about Y.)*

In what aspect of life do you feel pulled to make a difference? *(Look out there at the world; what bigger conversations matter to you?)*

Name three people whose lives you truly admire. *(Be aware of a tendency to make good-looking choices rather than authentic ones. Some people feel obliged to pick a parent or a spiritual leader.)* Next to their name, say what about their lives you would like to emulate.

If money were not an object, to what would you devote your life? *(Jot down at least twenty things. This is the "if I were given $5 million, what would I do with it" question, but that tends to provoke responses that are too materialistic for a mission.)*

Imagine looking back from age ninety. For what would you most like to be remembered?

A mission is a two- to three-sentence, present-tense statement of what you are about. Given everything you have just written, jot down possibilities and mull them over in the next twenty-four hours. Choose one. You can, and should, revise it if more insight presents itself.

Write your mission statement draft here:

Day 7 – Creating an inspiring vision

There are four different methods outlined in the text. "Be, Do, Have" is a three-column piece of paper or spreadsheet. The collage is best done on paper, as is the "conversation" exercise.

Here is a useful template for the "timeline" exercise. Make sure you change the domains on the top to yours that you created on Day 1. (You don't need all of them, but you definitely need the key ones.)

Another way to do this is with a flip chart and Post-it notes so you can move things around easily.

Year-end	Career	Job	Wellness	Finance	Home	Hobbies	Family	Spouse	Friends	
2040										
2030										
2025										
2020										
2016										
2015										
2014										
2013										

Day 8 – Your goals

For each "domain of success", write one to four goals that inspire you. A six- to eighteen-month timescale is about right for this.

Again, this is much easier in Excel or Evernote, but completing this in Word is adequate.

Goal	Measure	When	Status
Domain of success #1 (e.g., "Career")			
➤ **Goal 1**			
➤ **Goal 2**			
➤ **Goal 3**			

Day 9 – Turning goals into projects

Using the instructions given earlier, use your maximum creativity to create projects that will deliver your goals.

Goal	Projects
AREA (e.g., "Career")	
Extend my network in the publishing industry	Research and join best site
	Get introductions at two publishers
	Attend one writers workshop
Get on radar for Non-Exec appointments	Prepare resume version
	Research names of top head-hunters
	Create relationships with 5 head-hunters
Build personal brand	Give local TEDx talk
	Contribute twice weekly to LinkedIn discussions
	Attend media training

Reboot Your Life

	course

Day 10 – Turning projects into next actions

Here is a (live) sample of my goals to projects to next actions worksheet. Note that when two to three actions spring to mind, I place those "on deck."

Goals

Writing	Projects	Next Action	N + 1	N + 2
- Reboot published and sell 5000 copies	Manuscript/ cover	Review 80 pp	Send to BW	Cover spec
	Landing page	Draft LP	Autoresponder	
	PG site advertising	Draft Panel/ page		
	Financials ready	Amazon seller acct		
- Reboot repurposed for ADD/ Divorce/ Poker	Jan 31 start	Crowdsource next title		
- Why Change Fails draft completed	Ch 3	Mindmap ch	Research plan	
	Ch 4			
- WCF publisher found	Review proposal with MK	Schedule mtg		
- WCF agent found	Completed	Send contract		

Here is an MS Word table that you can use as your template. (Note: it is best to just paste your goal/project lists and make space for next actions.)

Goal	Project	Next Actions
Goal 1	Goal 1, Project A	Project A Next Action
	Goal 1, Project B	Project B Next Action
	Goal 1, Project C	Project C Next Action
Goal 2	Goal 2, Project A	Project A Next Action
	Goal 2, Project B	Project B Next

		Action

Because this can be confusing, I've included yet another example, that of getting the next promotion.

Goal	Project	Next Actions
Get promoted by end 2014	Review promotion criteria with manager. Unearth reservations and skill shortfalls.	1) *Reread job description for new role* 2) *Schedule time with manager* 3) *Agree upon mid-year progress review*
	Learn advanced project management	1) *Review internal and external programs* 2) *Get advice from HR* 3) *Schedule program*
	Get feedback from friends, peers, and network.	1) *List people whose feedback I value* 2) *Schedule 15m calls*

Each project has a sequence of actions because it is senseless to come up with them and not write them down. However, only one of those should go on your "Next Action" list. Never feel as if you must plan the entirety of your project in one sitting; sometimes only one step is clear.

Appendix 2 – Evernote Lists

This is a list of Evernote notes courtesy of the David Allen Company as a starter set.

- **Unprocessed** – the default folder where unprocessed items will go

- **Agendas** – lists of things to discuss with individuals

- **Areas of Focus** – lists of big-picture items that are your "North Star" to guide you

- **Calls** – list of the calls you need to make

- **Errands** – list of next actions you need to do outside of your home or office

- **Home** – list of next actions you have to physically do at home

- **Next Actions** – list of the next action you need to do in order to drive your projects toward "done"

- **Projects** – list of desired outcomes that require more than one action to complete

- **Reference** – list of items that you want to keep for future reference

- **Someday-Maybe** – list of ideas that you'd like to work on someday, but aren't committing to right now

- **Waiting For** – list of items that you have delegated or are waiting for someone else to do something about

Appendix 3 – List of resources

Getting Things Done: The Art of Stress-Free Productivity by David Allen (Penguin, 2001)

If you even modestly pursue what is within this book, you will find yourself much more productive. However, there are very high levels of personal mastery available. A "zero" inbox nightly? A working environment completely clear of stacks of papers to file and Post-it notes? All financial and other potentially threatening events handled long before they turn into problems? An eye on the five-year horizon, but terrific productivity in the moment? A head clear of distractions?

The David Allen Company (www.davidco.com) runs terrifically cost-effective workshops around the world that show where that greater productivity comes from.

The Seven Habits of Highly Effective People by Stephen Covey (Free Press, 1989)

Covey's first three habits—"Be Proactive," "Begin with the End in Mind," and "First Things, First"—are at the source of big-picture productivity. No better hundred pages have ever been written on how to lead a purposeful life.

Covey's business, Franklin Covey (www.franklincovey.com) offers training and productivity products for very reasonable costs.

Paul Gibbons

My website, launched September 2013, has a blog called *Leading Yourself* which will offer excerpts from this book and snips from upcoming books on personal leadership. It also has tools that support the process we have just learned under www.paulgibbons.net/RebootYourLife

My bigger commitment is to science-based leadership development and sustainable businesses. In the past few decades, we have learned a great deal about how the brain works and about how human beings function as a result. Little of that is yet in books on leadership and business.

As the world gets more complex, my assertion is that we cannot run 21st-century businesses using 20th-century science. My mission is to close that gap.

I would be delighted to keep in touch with tools, blogs, articles, and upcoming books, and we can do that through my community, which you can join at www.paulgibbons.net/sign-up.

Printed in Great Britain
by Amazon.co.uk, Ltd.,
Marston Gate.